The Poetry of Business Life

An Anthology

RALPH WINDLE

Berrett-Koehler Publishers
San Francisco

Berrett-Koehler Publishers, Inc.
155 Montgomery Street
San Francisco, CA 94104-4109
Tel: 415-288-0260   Fax: 415-362-2512

ORDERING INFORMATION

Individual sales. Berrett-Koehler publications are available through most bookstores. They can also be ordered direct from Berrett-Koehler at the address above.

Quantity sales. Special discounts are available on quantity purchases by corporations, associations, and others. For details, contact the "Special Sales Department" at the Berrett-Koehler address above.

Orders for college textbook/course adoption use. Please contact Berrett-Koehler Publishers at the address above.

Orders by U.S. trade bookstores and wholesalers. Please contact Publishers Group West, 4065 Hollis Street, Box 8843, Emeryville, CA 94662; Tel: 510-658-3453; 1-800-788-3123; Fax: 510-658-1834.

Orders in the U.K. and Western Europe. Please contact Probus Europe, 11 Millers Yard, Mill Lane, Cambridge CB2 1RG, England; Tel: 44-223-322018; Fax: 44-223-61149.

Printed in the United States of America

Printed on acid-free and recycled paper that meets the strictest state and U.S. guidelines for recycled paper (50 percent recycled waste, including 10 percent postconsumer waste).

Library of Congress Cataloging-in-Publication Data

The poetry of business life : an anthology / [compiled by] Ralph
    Windle. — 1st ed.
        p.   cm.

    Includes index.
    ISBN 1-881052-59-1
    1. Business—Poetry.   I. Windle, Ralph.

PN6110.B9P64   1994
808.81'9355—dc20
                                                                94-38199
                                                                    CIP

First Edition

99 98 97 96 95 94   10 9 8 7 6 5 4 3 2 1

To business that we love we rise betime,
And go to't with delight.
—Shakespeare
Antony and Cleopatra

O wad some Pow'r the giftie gie us
To see oursels as others see us!
It would frae mony a blunder free us,
And foolish notion...
—Robert Burns
To a Louse

To
JUSTIN and CHRISTINA
for
the rolling back of years.

Table of Contents

Canto II 𝕸oney

Canto III 𝕸arkets

Canto IV   Work

Canto V   Corporate Life

Canto VI   Comings and Goings

Canto VII Politics and Power

Canto VIII Technology and Change

Preface

"The Poetry of Business Life" is more than a title. It is an assertion and a challenge. "The Poetry of Love" would imply no such challenge, for Love is fully legitimate territory for poets, and has been since words were invented. Pets and Politics also qualify.

So what is different about Business? By now it touches most lives at work, store or home. It consumes growing proportions of our time, energies, ambitions and emotions. Its ideas and language, of markets and motivation, have become dominant in politics and social life. We are all, to some degree, in Business now, eagerly or reluctantly. Yet few, convention says, have sought inspiration or poetic challenge in its realities.

"Not many people in business feel an urge to write verse about their work," wrote Alan Farnham in *Fortune* (February 1991), thus providing a final stimulus for this book. "Good poems about business are grievously thin on the ground," wrote Godfrey Smith in the Sunday *Times* (of London), "and serious ones, I should have thought, non-existent." Both, I am happy to add, have been sporting allies in this attempt to prove otherwise.

In this book over seventy writers, and twice that many pieces, supply the evidence that there is a "Poetry of Business Life." Not only is it alive and well, but it also draws on a longer, mainstream poetic tradition. Why that should be so, and why poetic language seems, against the odds, ripe to push its relevance deeper into the business experience, I touch on in my Introduction.

Three years, and much collective enterprise, were needed not only to cull the best of what might already exist in the literature, but to encourage out many previously unpublished or comparatively unknown writers, in and around the business world. My problem became one of exclusion rather than inclusion. Work from contemporary business writers, responding to my appeal, outstrips by many times the space I have. Many others in business suggested established work which had, in some important way, influenced them. The project evoked a heartwarming interest and support from many individuals in the business, media and literary communities (see Acknowledgements).

After a short retrospective (Canto I: Origins) I have chosen to allow new writers to jostle with established ones, the famous with the less-known, speaking their poetry side-by-side and directly to you the reader. Everyone with whom I have shared a preliminary reading has found these pieces compulsive, stunning and, above all, enjoyable—for their exuberant diversity, pathos, humor and occasional anger. Beyond that, their quality of expression and uninhibited insights collectively produce an unprecendented and challenging picture of business life as it emerges from its past and moves toward a new millennium.

Ralph Windle
Oxford, England
September 1994

Acknowledgments

My first thanks must go to the many writers, published and previously unpublished, whose creativity makes this book. Below I make more formal acknowledgments of sources, copyrights and permissions, where these are due.

My gratitude extends much wider, however, and not least to those many other writers in business, by far the majority, who submitted work for which I could find no space. I encourage them to persist, and thank them for being part of the wide, and still expanding, network of enthusiastic people who turned a modest project into an exciting adventure.

Much of this I owe to a small but influential group of people who gave moral support to the concept before there was much to show, including Sir Peter Parker, Professor Charles Handy and, in the United States of America, James Autry. These were later joined by Howard Davies, director general of the Confederation of British Industry, and Christine Large of Epigram Associates. Christine rapidly moved beyond moral to active support, involving the media and many others in propagating the idea.

I have already acknowledged the role of Alan Farnham (*Fortune*) and Godfrey Smith (the Sunday *Times* of London) in goading me on. In broadening the appeal to people in business, Gay Haskins, director general of the European Foundation for Management Development in Brussels, was proactive in spreading the message into continental Europe. Many corporations in different parts of the world also embraced the appeal.

When energy or morale occasionally flagged, however, I was able to turn for advice, encouragement and much wisdom, to four special people—James Autry, Harry Newman, Jr., and Dana Gioia in the United States, and Michael Ivens in the United Kingdom. The existence and special qualities of this book owe much to them.

Steven Piersanti and his splendid team at Berrett-Koehler Publishers, Inc., have performed miracles of editing and design for a distant but grateful author. My own team, whose motto has become *fax nobiscum*, has performed equal wonders: Terry Allison at the word processor, Val Glenn with permissions, and a host of other enthusiasts.

My greatest and most consistent debt is to my family, for what might have been too many hours of neglect. My wife Ariana, however, caught the infection of this project too, and you will see her designs on the canto title pages inside the book.

The editor and publishers gratefully acknowledge the sources and permissions to reproduce copyright poems in this book.

Constance Alexander and the University of Phoenix Press: for permission to reprint "Outplacement Blues."

David Alpaugh: for permission to reprint "A California Ad Man Celebrates His Art" from *Counterpoint*. Brownsville, Oregon: Stork Line Press, 1994. Copyright David Alpaugh, 1994.

W. H. Auden: "The Managers" from *Collected Shorter Poems*

1927–1957. Reprinted by permission of Faber and Faber Ltd. and Random House, Inc.

James A. Autry: for permission to reprint "Dialogue with the Past," "What to Know about Hanging On," "Lights Flashing at O'Hare," "On Firing a Salesman" and "Recessions" from *Love and Profit* (William Morrow, 1991); and "Genealogy" and "Off Again" from *Nights under a Tin Roof* (Yoknapatawpha Press, 1983).

Stafford Beer: "Boardroom" from *Transit* (Charlottetown, 1983). Copyright Stafford Beer.

Kate Bertrand and the University of Phoenix Press: for permission to reprint "Racing with the Wolves."

John Betjeman: John Murray (Publishers) Limited for permission to reprint "Executive," "The City," "Business Girls" and "Variation on a Theme by Newbolt" from *John Betjeman, Collected Poems 1988*.

Geoffrey Bownas: for permission to reprint translations of poems by Takenaka Iku and Nakahara Chuya from *The Penguin Book of Japanese Verse* (1964). Editors Geoffrey Bownas and Anthony Thwaite.

Basil Bunting: "What the Chairman Told Tom" from *The Complete Poems* (Oxford University Press, 1994). Copyright The Estate of Basil Bunting, 1994. Reprinted by permission of Oxford University Press.

Geoffrey Chaucer: from "The Prologue" to *The Canterbury Tales* translated by Nevill Coghill (Penguin Classics, 1951, fourth revised edition, 1977). Copyright Nevill Coghill, 1951, 1958, 1960, 1975, 1977. Reprinted by permission of Penguin Books Ltd.

Wendy Cope: "Engineers' Corner" from *Making Cocoa for Kingsley Amis*. Reprinted by permission of Faber & Faber Ltd.

E. E. Cummings: "a salesman is an it ..." and "Poem, or Beauty Hurts Mr. Vinal" from *Complete Poems*. Reprinted by permission of W. W. Norton.

Donald Davie: "Thanks to Industrial Essex" from *Essex Poems*. Copyright Donald Davie, 1986.

Gavin Ewart: for permission to reprint "Advertising Elegiacs" and "Happiness Is Girl-Shaped" from *Gavin Ewart: Collected Poems 1980–90* (Century Hutchinson, 1991); and his "The Caged Copywriter."

Dana Gioia: "Money," copyright 1991 by Dana Gioia. Reprinted from *The Gods of Winter* with the permission of Graywolf Press, Saint Paul, Minnesota. "The Man in the Open Doorway" and "In Cheever Country," copyright 1986 by Dana Gioia. Reprinted from *Daily Horoscope* with the permission of Graywolf Press, Saint Paul, Minnesota.

Emily Hawthorne and the University of Phoenix Press: for permission to reprint "Merrill Lynch."

Lindsay Hill: "Taking up Serpents (Chicago Board of Trade)." Copyright Lindsay Hill.

Kenneth Ho: for permission to reprint lines from *The Nineteen Ancient Poems*, translated from the Chinese by Kenneth Ho. (Kelly and Walsh, Hong Kong, 1977).

Anselm Hollo: for permission to reprint poems by Paavo Haavikko from *Paavo Haavikko: Selected Poems*, translated from the Finnish by Anselm Hollo (Carcanet Press Limited, 1991). Copyright 1991 by Paavo Haavikko (poems) and Anselm Hollo (translations).

Carolyn Hull: "Where Does the Money Go" and "Declining the Loan" from *The Literature of Work* (University of Phoenix Press, 1991).

Michael Ivens: for permission to reprint "Don Juan in a Dark Suit," "Pending," "Jenkins Is A-Weeping" and "Dead Factory at Night" from *Private and Public* (Villiers, 1963) and *Another Sky* (Villiers, 1968).

Natasha Josefowitz and Columbus Books: "I Have Arrived" and "The Executive's Wife" from *Is This Where I Was Going?* (Columbus Books, 1986). Copyright Natasha Josefowitz, 1983.

Dr. Fritz Kornfeld: for permission to reprint "The Jubilar," translated from the German by Inge Adams and Ralph Windle. Copyright Dr. Fritz Kornfeld, Essen, Germany.

Kajetan Kovic: "Robots" in *The Penguin Book of Socialist Verse (1970)*. Copyright Kajetan Kovic, 1970.

Philip Larkin: "Toads" from *Collected Poems*. Reprinted by permission of Faber & Faber Ltd.

George MacBeth: Sheil Land Associates Ltd. for permission to reprint "The Miner's Helmet" from *George MacBeth: Collected Poems 1958–82* (Century Hutchinson, 1989). Copyright George Mac-Beth, 1989.

John Marsh: pieces from *Late Glimpses* by John Marsh, C.B.E. Reprinted by permission of Mrs. Mary Marsh.

Ogden Nash: "Bankers Are Just Like Anybody Else, Except Richer,"* "We Would Refer You to Our Service Department, If We Had One"** and "Kindly Unhitch That Star, Buddy" all from *Verses from 1929 On* by Ogden Nash. Copyright 1935, 1948 by Ogden Nash. "The Banker's Special" from *Versus* by Ogden

*First appeared in *The New Yorker*.
**First appeared in *Promenade*.

Nash. Copyright 1949 by Ogden Nash. By permission of Little, Brown & Company and Curtis Brown Ltd.

Pablo Neruda: "The United Fruit Co.," translation copyright Robert Bly, from *The Faber Book of Political Verse* (1986).

Harry Newman, Jr.: for permission to reprint "VIP, A Conversation," "Testimonial," "Awake," "What Do You Want to Hear?," "Aging Jet Setter," "Survival Kit," "Business Friends" and "Out of Synch" from *Behind Pinstripes* (Tamas and Brownson, 1984) and *Poems for Executives and Other Addicts.* Copyright Harry Newman, Jr., Chairman, Newman Properties, Long Beach, California.

Charles Blackburn Owen: for permission to reprint "Underground Press," "City Leak," "Golden Mean," "Business Connection" and "Commuter Platform." Copyright Charles Blackburn Owen, 1994.

William Oxley: for permission to reprint lines from *Playboy* (University of Salzburg Press, 1992); and "Really England's," "Out of Place" and "Social Comment." Copyright William Oxley.

P. K. Page: for permission to reprint "The Stenographers" from *The Penguin Book of Canadian Verse.* Edited by Ralph Gustafson, 1958. Copyright P. K. Page, 1946.

Peter Porter and the Oxford University Press: for permission to reprint "A Consumer's Report," "Inspector Christopher Smart Calls," "Print Out: Apocalypse," and lines from "Shopping Scenes" from *Peter Porter's Collected Poems* (Oxford University Press, 1983). Copyright Peter Porter, 1983.

Jonathan Price: "Waiting" from *The Literature of Work* (Phoenix University Press, 1991).

Theodore Roethke: "Dolor," copyright 1943 by Modern Poetry Association, Inc., from *The Collected Poems of Theodore Roethke.* Used by permission of Doubleday, a division of Bantam Doubleday Dell Publishing Group, Inc., and Faber & Faber Ltd.

Vita Sackville-West: "Craftsmen" from *The Land.* Copyright Nigel Nicolson and reprinted with his permission.

Dr. Lothar Schmidt: for permission to print "Aphorisms," translated from the German by Inge Adams and Ralph Windle, from *Rotary Aphorisms.* Copyright Dr. Lothar Schmidt, Friedrichsdorf, Germany.

Floyd Skloot: for permission to reprint "A Working Marriage" from *Music Appreciation* (University of Central Florida Contemporary Poetry Series, University Press of Florida, 1994); and "I Am Getting a Mountain View," published in *Phantasm,* spring 1979.

Brian Smith: for permission to reprint pieces from *Sketching in Verse.* Copyright Brian Smith.

Patrick Taylor: for permission to reprint "Bankrupt" from *A View from Suburbia* (National Poetry Foundation, 1992).

Ralph Windle and Bertie Ramifications Limited: for permission to reprint poems from *The Bottom Line* (Century Hutchinson, 1985) and *Boardroom Ballads* (Adler and Adler, USA, 1986).

Great care has been taken by the editor to trace and give correct attribution for quoted work in this anthology. I apologize for any inadvertent errors which, on notification, will be corrected in future printings.

Introduction

The Western Myth of Managerial Man (and Woman) is one of the dominant myths of our Age—testimony to the pervasiveness and power of Business. It has selected those human attributes thought relevant to executive success in the structured Corporation, especially competitive ambition and financial numeracy; and groomed many generations, through business school and other institutions, in the techniques and attitudes thought appropriate to this corporate behavioral need.

Of less apparent relevance to this prescribed model were some other important and, some argued, more basic human attributes, related to emotional needs and wider family, social and intellectual aspirations and relationships. The need to reconcile these competing demands, of the corporate and the fuller life, has stimulated new discussion in a renascent business literature, questioning the "Myth." James Autry, Harry Newman, and many others in this anthology focus on the prevailing tensions caused by it. It is not an accident that many should turn to poetry to do so.

For the conventional language of business itself, as Roy Doughty has accurately observed, is predominantly the language of information—accounting, policy manuals, financial reports—aimed at "delineating, defining, separating" for the purposes of measurement and control. It is a technical language, honed to its specific purpose, but constrained in wider, more complex applications.

As Doughty continues, "The language of poetry is the language of evocation. . . . The language of information says something about objects, but the language of evocation speaks about relationships. Poetry is as precise and effective in the realms of relationships as the language of accounting is in the realm of finance. Business people also need this language because the world of commerce, no less than the worlds of ecology and spirit, is a nest of inter-relatedness."

Development of richer poetic language in the business world requires, and provokes, one further challenge—the rescue of business from the narrowing constraints being put on its meaning and application. For what is business anyway? It's a good Old English word (*bisignis:* busy-ness) that has been progressively wrenched away from its core meanings—task, work, occupation, profession, trade—toward the narrower concepts of dealing, buying, selling. Now, more recently, it has been virtually hijacked for the even narrower financial and accounting veneer of these honorable business activities. We need "business" back for all that richer diversity of activities by which we barter our work and skills, however modest, for our pittances. Tycoons and Top People are not the only ones in "business" even though, in the age of the image-makers and the business pages, they are obtrusively dominant.

"Business," in this broader sense, and its poetry, pre-dates by many centuries the Corporation, Henry Ford and even the East India Company and Industrial Revolution. Sa'adi, the Persian poet, died in 1291 but bequeathed to all businessmen to come the poignant epitaph:

> The luck of wealth dependeth not on skill,
> But only on the aid of Heaven's will:
> So has it happened since the world began—
> The witless ape outstrips the learned man.

Women aspirants for business had their poetic champion in Agathias, many centuries before the Equal Opportunities Commissions. Martial, a Latin-speaking emigrant from Spain to Rome in 64 A.D., explained the banker's lending psychology long ago:

> 'Tis hard refusing when you're asked to lend;
> But to refuse before you're asked displays
> Inventive genius worthy of the bays!

Money, wealth and escape from poverty—arch motivators of business enterprise—are recurring themes in poetic literature from the Nineteen Ancient Chinese Poems of 300 B.C.; and stimulated their first great epic drama in Shakespeare's *The Merchant of Venice*.

There were poets around when the industrial revolutions, starting about 1760 in England, spread the technologies of machine and production engineering around the world and shaped "business" and the "corporation" toward their now familiar forms. One such poet, Edward Young (1683–1765), even lays claim to be father of business verse (see Canto I: Origins), but is better remembered for the message on many an office wall—"Procrastination is the thief of time."

So the more modern and contemporary poets who dominate this anthology inherit a poetic language which, even in the subject matter of business, has a long and rich tradition. The "globality" which many now claim for business is an infant compared to the "global" reach of poetry's idiom.

In more recent times, it was again a poet who drew attention to another distinction—central to current discussion of business life—between the archetypal "businessman" of literature (entrepreneur, free-actor, risk-taker) and the emerging "professional corporate manager." It was W. H. Auden in *The Managers*.

> In the bad old days it was not so bad:
>   The top of the ladder
> Was an amusing place to sit; success
>   Meant quite a lot—leisure
> And huge meals, more palaces filled with more
>   Objects, books, girls, horses
> Than one would ever get round to, . . .

. . . .

> The last word on how we may live or die
>> Rests today with such quiet
> Men, working too hard in rooms that are too big,
>> Reducing to figures
> What is the matter, what is to be done. . . .

For most professional managers are now "businessmen" only in the broadest, colloquial sense of the word. Even with the occasional share option, and however senior, most are the hired craftsmen and journeymen of business, not the assumed plutocratic "owners" with whom society often identifies them.

Auden, with no evident life connection with "business," joins those "outsider" poets in this anthology—Ogden Nash, G. K. Chesterton, John Betjeman, Philip Larkin and others—who have pungently commented on it.

Since business has now absorbed or replaced so many occupations which support a living, it would be a devastating blow to poetry itself if the poets found neither place nor inspiration in it. Many of our most prominent twentieth century poets, even where they have not explored its subject matter, have worked in business with no apparent fatal damage to their muse. Since this anthology has business as its subject, we are the losers by it.

As Dana Gioia (one of the finest of contemporary American poets and a late marketing vice president of General Foods) has reminded us, we might otherwise have included T. S. Eliot, A. R. Ammons, Wallace Stevens, James Dickey in this collection. To which I could add Walter de la Mare, Roy Fuller and many others. Even with these poets of genius, however, who made little direct allusion to their business lives, imagery from that life occasionally breaks through. I see some of it in T. S. Eliot (the "Unreal City" of *The Waste Land*) and, in lesser moments, it bubbles out:

> I shall not want Capital in Heaven,
>> For I shall meet Sir Alfred Mond.
> We two shall live together, lapt
>> In a five per cent Exchequer Bond.

Our eyes, however, are inevitably drawn to the "Business Poets" in both senses of the phrase: those who work, or have worked, in "business" and have chosen—occasionally or more continuously—to write about it. This draws on a rich mixture of "professional" poets—in the sense that they have published works and are more easily accessible; and newer, sometimes "unpublished" writers. Among the latter, there is a refreshing incidence of women writers.

Among the well-known "professional" poets, both Gavin Ewart and Peter Porter have seen business through the prism of the advertising agency where, presumably, the "creative" facility with words has its most direct business utility.

Michael Ivens has had and retained a wider business interest, to match his poetic one, and his *Jenkins Is A-Weeping* has the immediate, authentic stamp of someone who has been there:

> Unaccustomed as he was
> To public speaking, laughing, crying, dancing,
> Singing, or other extravagances
> Better left undone, or second best,
> Released in the private bar or in the home,
> He found that,
>   "Retirement is a bit of a shock,
> I'm going to miss all my colleagues and friends,
> And thank you so much for this wonderful clock
> And..."
>   Heard a curious song
>   And stopped.

No one has articulated the dilemmas of the contemporary manager-poet better than Dana Gioia. His pieces, reproduced here from *The Gods of Winter* and *Daily Horoscope*, are rare direct comments on his business life within the totality of those collections. My dialogue with Dana Gioia, on poetry and business, has been a major stimulus to this book.

The most committed and highly influential "poetry-in-business" voice is that of James Autry—until recently president of the Magazine Group of the Meredith Corporation in the United States.

His recent book, *Love and Profit,* is—with its unique mixture of
verse and prose—a cogent, but unsentimental, plea for the release of
the emotions in the corporate workplace.

Less well known may be some of Autry's earlier pieces (from
Nights under a Tin Roof and *Life after Mississippi*), but I find them
unique in their biographical tracing of the successful business exec-
utive to the young Tennessee boy in a different time and place.

> You are
> in these hills
> who you were and who you will become
> and not just who you are
>> *She was a McKinstry*
>> *and his mother was a Smith*
>
> . . . .
>
> In other times and other places
> there are new families and new names
>> *He's ex P & G*
>> *out of Benton and Bowles*
>> *and was brand management with Colgate*
>
> And listeners sip Dewar's and soda or puff New True Lights
> and know how people will do things
> they are expected to do . . .

The combination of "successful property developer" and "prom-
inent businessman" strains most conventional assumptions about
"the poet." Harry Newman, Jr., chairman of a Long Beach, Cali-
fornia, property company, is all three. Inside his collection, *Behind
Pinstripes,* is the evidence of the impressive, highly sensitive poet,
with the courage to examine the complex costs of business success—
for love, family, friends—as the downside of its exhilarations.

> Eat your vitamins
> Jog three times a week
> Work out at the gym
> Follow that salt-free
> Low-cholesterol diet
> Religiously

Bend all your efforts
To survive
And in the process
You will forget about
Living

Inevitably I have had to look to translation to discover how far these business allusions are replicated elsewhere. They are—and you will find glimpses of how Finnish, German, Japanese and other poets have reacted to the same phenomenon.

In the lively and developing Poetry of Business Life it is the newer (i.e., less published) work on which the case ultimately rests. Here, touching only its fringe, I find the evidence of many contemporary younger writers—men and women—producing energetic, marvelously diverse and assured work on many aspects of this life. They come to it with the poet's essentially idiosyncratic motivation and voice. Equally exciting is my evidence of how many of their "older" business colleagues have been at this process, privately and unnoticed, for a very long time.

Function and status within the business organization seem irrelevant to the poetic urge. Banker, engineer, computer technician, accountant, personnel executive, consultant, marketeer—all are included. Secretary, midrank executive and chairman rub shoulders. From many a well-known business name verse emerges as the reflective companion of distinguished careers: John Marsh, a former director of the British Institute of Management who has sadly died during the process of compilation; Dr. Lothar Schmidt, prominent Frankfurt economist and financial adviser; Sir Jeremy Morse, former chairman of Lloyds Bank; Brian Smith, former chief executive of P.A. Consulting International.

I offer the reader some rough map references for a first journey through the anthology in the form of eight subject "Cantos." They can, and should, be progressively discarded as you grow familiar with the book's territory. A good poem may hold a universe of meaning and most of these pieces could leap easily across these arbitrary boundaries, between one reading and another. Among the Canto topics chosen, however, one ("Comings and Goings") illustrates

one of many exhilarating surprises I have had in the compilation.
Travel proves to be a major topic for contemporary business poets
and, whether commuting or distant journeys, symbolizes for many
the way business extends its grip beyond the office door.

Charles Blackburn Owen has it well, compressing in this meta-
phor much of what recurs in this anthology:

> Divided love, divided care,
> Synthesized at half-past eight,
> Urgency is down the stair,
> Through the door and garden gate.
> Platform One, time to spare
> To corner, kill the rebel thought,
> To love your neighbour, to compare
> His shadow pale or long or short,
> A half-way house to nowhere new,
> A precognition of decay
> Before the hearse that bears us to
> Another unheroic day.

Except in Canto I: Origins nothing else will intervene between
poet and reader. I envy you that first sharp kick of pleasure, pi-
quancy and surprise which all good cocktails provide and of which
I had the privileged first taste. As Joseph Joubert said, "You will find
poetry nowhere unless you bring some of it with you." I hope that
you are about to rediscover that there are many, in and around the
Business Life, who meet at least that condition.

Canto I

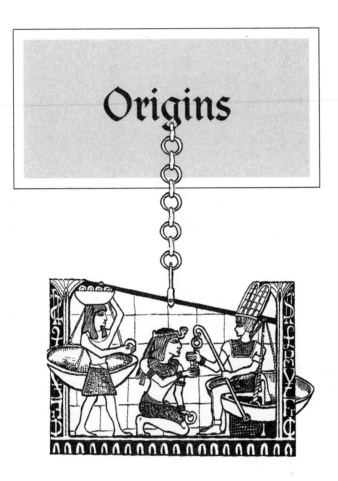

The thing that hath been, it is that which shall be;
and that which is done is that which shall be done:
there is no new thing under the sun.
—The Bible, *Ecclesiastes*

Lady Luck: The Patron Saint of Business?

SA'ADI
Persian   c. 1200 A.D.

If livelihood by knowledge were endowed,
None would be poorer than the brainless crowd;
Yet Fortune on the fool bestows the prize,
And leaves but themes for wonder to the wise.

The luck of wealth dependeth not on skill,
But only on the aid of Heaven's will:
So has it happened since the world began—
The witless ape outstrips the learned man.
A poet dies of hunger, grief, and cold;
A fool among the ruins findeth gold.

Sa'adi's thirteenth century conclusion, still shared by many, had already two thousand years of literature on which to draw.

In the long history of homo sapiens (as he ironically named himself) writing comes late and printing is a mere babe-in-arms. The poet spoke, long before he wrote; and his audience listened before it read. When the new technology of writing was invented, many of the themes, cadences and rhythms of poetry had long been honed by the performing bard on an uncouth and earthy live audience, fresh from the fields and the grinding labor of survival. So, even in those few surviving fragments of the early poets with a pen, the *business* of living—seeking success, escaping poverty, making money— is there, already on the poet's agenda.

from The Panchatantra

ANONYMOUS
Sanskrit   c. 200 B.C.

A beggar to the graveyard hied
And there "Friend corpse, arise" he cried;
"One moment lift my heavy weight
Of poverty; for I of late

Grow weary, and desire instead
Your comfort; you are good and dead."
The corpse was silent. He was sure
'Twas better to be dead than poor.

Translated from the Sanskrit by Arthur W. Ryder

To the ancient Chinese poet, the spirit of enterprise was a better response. Here is the first exhortation to "get up and go" to find success and enjoy its fruits.

from The Nineteen Ancient Poems

ANONYMOUS
Chinese   c. 300 B.C.

Today we enjoy a splendid feast:
Its pleasures and delights are beyond describing.
Play on the lute sounds of surpassing sweetness,
Melodies new, beauty distilled from heaven.
Skilful singers intone the fine word;
Recognising the song the hearers will understand.

For the wishes of all are the same
Though our desires may remain unspoken.
Man lodges in the world for a single lifetime,
Suddenly passing away like a swirl of dust.
So, why not spur your courser on,
Be ahead at the highway and the ford?

Do not stay poor and unhonoured
And endure a long life of sorrow.

Translated from the Chinese by Kenneth Ho

Then, as now, there were complaints that the dice were loaded in the business-of-life game. Women noticed early.

from The Greek Anthology

AGATHIAS
Greek c. 500 A.D.

Not such your burden, happy youths, as ours—
  Poor women children nurtured daintily—
For ye have comrades when ill-fortune lours,
  To hearten you with talk and company;
And ye have games for solace, and may roam
  Along the streets and see the painters' shows.
But woe betide us if we stir from home—
  And there our thoughts are dull enough, God knows!

Translated from the Greek by William M. Hardinge

At the height of the Athenian democracy and empire in the fifth
century B.C., business and commerce were much more sophisti-
cated. Offshore investment was growing; litigation and taxation
were big political themes. Aristophanes, a possible contributor of
business satire to the *Wall Street Journal*, would have felt totally at
home in contemporary New York and London. Here he writes on
the peace dividend and defense industry when the "hot war" be-
tween Athens and Sparta temporarily cooled.

from The Peace

ARISTOPHANES
Greek c. 444–380 B.C.

Chorus: Back to dear, old Blighty, chaps,
        Put up the aching feet.
      Hang up the army-issue caps
        Some decent grub to eat.
      For when it comes to battle I'm
        Bravest when it ends;
      I'm more for peaceful drinking time
        All cosy with my friends.

Scythe-maker:	Dear old Trygaeus! what you've done
	   For business with this Peace!
	My sickles wouldn't fetch a cent.
	   Now they're a grand apiece!

Weapon Salesman:	Ye gods. I'm ruined! Helmets, spears,
	   My weapon stock's as deep as Hell;
	It's bankruptcy for us when Peace
	   Makes war on us with arms to sell!

Translated from the Greek by Ralph Windle

Heavy rods of iron were, reputedly, the earliest form of unwieldy money, when barter was no longer enough. Coinage soon followed, however, to oil the wheels of trade; and with it came the moneylender, usurer, banker and all subsequent dealers in interest, promissory notes and "futures."

From Sextus the Usurer — The Epigrams

MARTIAL
Roman c. 40–104 A.D.

Whenever he observes me purchasing
A cloak, a slave, or any suchlike thing,
Sextus the usurer—a man, you know,
Who's been my friend for twenty years or so—
In fear that I may ask him for a loan
Thus whispers, to himself, but in a tone
Such as he knows I cannot choose but hear:
"I owe Secundus twenty thousand clear,
I owe Phileus thirty thousand more,
And then there's Phoebus—that's another four—
Besides, there's interest due on each amount;
And not a farthing in my bank account!"
O stratagem profound of my old friend!
'Tis hard refusing when you're asked to lend;
But to refuse before you're asked displays
Inventive genius worthy of the bays!

Translated from the Latin by Kirby Flower Smith

We still look back at the golden age of Rome as a golden age of poetry. Not all of the poets—Virgil, Horace and others—were rhapsodizing, like Catullus, about his loves. Horace was bemoaning a cosmopolitan Rome, already overrun with lawyers and businessmen, where moneymaking was in conflict with the old virtues.

From Epistles: Book 1

HORACE
Roman   65–8 B.C.

Why doubt that virtue counts for more than gold?
"Seek money first, good friends, and virtue next,"
Each Janus lectures on the well-worn text;
Lads learn it at their lessons: grey-haired men,
Like school-boys, drawl the sing-song o'er again.

But mark these children at their play; they sing,
"Deal fairly, youngster, and we'll crown you king."

Which is the better teacher, tell me, pray,
The law of Grabbit, or the children's lay
That crowns fair dealing, by Camillus trolled,
Or manly Curius, in the days of old:
The voice that says, "Make money, money, man;
Honestly, if may be—if not, which way you can?"

Suppose the world of Rome accosts me thus:
"You walk where we walk; why not think like us,
Join us for better or for worse, pursue
The things we love, and those we don't eschew?"

We leap a thousand years, as anthologists can, to more familiar writers and times—but still short of the industrial revolutions which shaped the business we now know. The poor are still with us, striving to get out, but the merchant and the trader have more clearly emerged as the archetypal businessmen.

from The Prologue to The Canterbury Tales

GEOFFREY CHAUCER
1340–1400 A.D.

There was a Merchant with a forking beard
And motley dress: high on his horse he sat,
Upon his head a Flemish beaver hat
And on his feet daintily buckled boots.
He told of his opinions and pursuits
In solemn tones, and how he never lost.
The sea should be kept free at any cost
(He thought) upon the Harwich-Holland ranges.
He was expert at dabbling in exchanges.
This estimable Merchant so had set
His wits to work, none knew he was in debt,
He was so stately in negotiation,
Loan, bargain and commercial obligation.
He was an excellent fellow all the same;
To tell the truth I do not know his name.

Modern English version by Nevill Coghill

The surest, if regrettable, sign of how deeply business, money and
the power they wield can penetrate human emotions is when these
themes surface in tragic poetry. This was to happen, first and most
significantly, in Shakespeare's *The Merchant of Venice*, where the
banal language of transactions becomes a metaphor for human rela-
tionships, prejudice and misunderstandings.

The Merchant of Venice (passim)

WILLIAM SHAKESPEARE
1564–1616

I will buy with you, sell with you,
Talk with you, walk with you, and so following;
But I will not eat with you, drink with you,
Nor pray with you. What news on the Rialto?

. . . .

I hate him for he is a Christian;
But more for that in low simplicity
He lends out money gratis, and brings down
The rate of usance here with us in Venice.
If I can catch him once upon the hip,
I will feed fat the ancient grudge I bear him.
He hates our sacred nation, and he rails
Even there where merchants most do congregate,
On me, my bargains, and my well-won thrift,
Which he calls interest.

. . . .

    Men that hazard all
Do it in hope of fair advantages:
A golden mind stoops not to show of dross.

. . . .

There is some ill a-brewing towards my rest.
For I did dream of money-bags tonight.

. . . .

Nay, take my life and all; pardon not that:
You take my house when you do take the prop
That doth sustain my house; you take my life
When you do take the means whereby I live.

The shattering impact of industrialization on life, and business as
it was to be, came with the Industrial Revolution—first in England
(about 1740) and then rapidly in America and continental Europe.
Its first poets responded with a—happily short-lived—heroic age
hyperbole, eminently forgettable except for its curiosity value and
delightful humbug. Preeminent was Edward Young, elsewhere ca-
pable of better things, who lodged the claim to be the world's first
"business poet."

From Imperium Pelagi, or The Merchant

EDWARD YOUNG
1683–1765

Thee, Trade! I first—who boast no store,
Who owe thee nought—thus snatch from shore,

The shore of Prose, where thou has slumbered long;
   And send thy flag triumphant down
   The tide of time to sure renown.
O bless my country! and thou pay'st my song. . . .

   Is "merchant" an inglorious name?
   No; fit for Pindar such a theme;
Too great for me; I pant beneath the weight.
   If loud as Ocean were my voice,
   If words and thoughts to court my choice
Outnumber'd sands, I could not reach its height.

   Merchants o'er proudest heroes reign;
   Those trade in blessing, these in pain,
At slaughter swell, and shout while nations groan.
   With purple monarchs merchants vie;
   If great to spend, what to supply?
Priests pray for blessings; merchants pour them down.

   Kings, merchants are in league and love,
   Earth's odours pay soft airs above,
That o'er the teeming field prolific range.
   Planets are merchants; take, return,
   Lustre and heat; by traffic burn;
The whole creation is one vast Exchange. . . .

Ode

Sung at the Opening of the International Exhibition

ALFRED LORD TENNYSON
1809–1892

Uplift a thousand voices full and sweet
   In this wide hall with earth's invention stored,
   And praise the invisible universal Lord,
Who lets once more in peace the nations meet,
   Where Science, Art, and Labour have outpour'd
Their myriad horns of plenty at our feet.

O ye, the wise who think, the wise who reign,
From growing commerce loose her latest chain,
And let the fair white-wing'd peacemaker fly
To happy havens under all the sky,
And mix the seasons and the golden hours;
Till each man find his own in all men's good,
And all men work in noble brotherhood,
Breaking their mailed fleets and armed towers,
And ruling by obeying Nature's powers,
And gathering all the fruits of earth and crown'd
    with all her flowers.

Manufacturing technology moved fast. James Watt, the great Scottish engineer, inventor and machine manufacturer, himself turned to verse in the exuberance of another deal satisfactorily concluded!

Letter to Matthew Boulton June 30, 1779

JAMES WATT
1736–1819

Birmingham

Hallelujah! Hallelujee!
We have concluded with Hawkesbury,
2171. per annum from Lady-day last;
2751.5s. for time past; 1571. on account.
We make them a present of 100 guineas—
Peace and good-fellowship on earth—
Perrins and Evans to be dismissed—
3 more engines wanted in Cornwall—
Dudley repentant and amendant—
                    Yours rejoicing
                    JAMES WATT

In the hot ferment of ideas, there were even poets to argue the case for state financial involvement in business development.

From Science Revealed

GEORGE EVERLEIGH
c. 1865

If, then, the State will but assistance lend
To give security to Companies,
The Public Companies with monied wings
Will fly like eagles to the scent of prey,
And every nook and corner of the world
Will find its Companies of men at work;
And, for the aid each Company receives,
Each Company could well afford to pay,
Out of its surplus revenues, the State;
If out of three but two a surplus have,
Two-thirds of each will reimburse the State,
And hold one-third a bonus to account,
Which gives the State two-thirds for profit too,
And two to reimburse the one that's lost.
Thus, if a Government agrees to give,
Whenever Public Companies are formed,
To each a dividend—say, six per cent
Per annum for a certain fixed time,
And for security inspects accounts—
Then, of the profits which each yieldeth more
Than the same dividend of six per cent,
Two-thirds the Government itself shall claim,
The other third remaining to afford
The Company an extra dividend.

Better things were to come! The Industrial Revolution marks the point in history where business began to take on the shape, themes and forms with which we are familiar. The comments of many mainstream poets, whose names and work speak fully for themselves, comprise the rest of this collection.

Canto II

Money

Money is a kind of poetry...
—Wallace Stevens

There is no money in poetry, but then
there's no poetry in money either....
—Robert Graves

I'm tired of Love: I'm still more tired of Rhyme.
But Money gives me pleasure all the time.
—Hilaire Belloc

Money

DANA GIOIA

Money, the long green,
cash, stash, rhino, jack
or just plain dough.

Chock it up, fork it over,
shell it out. Watch it
burn holes through pockets.

To be made of it! To have it
to burn! Greenbacks, double eagles,
megabucks and Ginnie Maes.

It greases the palm, feathers a nest,
holds heads above water,
makes both ends meet.

Money breeds money.
Gathering interest, compounding daily.
Always in circulation.

Money. You don't know where it's been,
but you put it where your mouth is.
And it talks.

Tourist Japan

TAKENAKA IKU

FUJIYAMA—we sell.
Miyajima—we sell.
Nikkö—we sell.
Japan—we sell anywhere.
Naruto, Aso—
We sell it all.
Prease, prease, come and view!

Me rub hands,
Put on smile,
Money, money—that's the thing!
We Japanese   all buy cars
We Japanese   all like lighters
We Japanese   all good gardeners
We Japanese   all sing pops.
All of us bow,
All, all, are meek and mild. Yes!

Translated from the Japanese by Geoffrey Bownas

Bankers Are Just Like Anybody Else, Except Richer

OGDEN NASH

This is a song to celebrate banks.
Because they are full of money and you go into them and
    all you hear is clinks and clanks.
Or maybe a sound like the wind in the trees on the hills,
Which is the rustling of the thousand dollar bills.
Most bankers dwell in marble halls,
Which they get to dwell in because they encourage
    deposits and discourage withdralls.
And particularly because they all observe one rule which
    woe betides the banker who fails to heed it,
Which is you must never lend any money to anybody unless
    they don't need it.
I know you, you cautious conservative banks!
If people are worried about their rent it is your duty to
    deny them the loan of one nickel, yes, even one
    copper engraving of the martyred son of the late
    Nancy Hanks;
Yes, if they request fifty dollars to pay for a baby you
    must look at them like Tarzan looking at an uppity
    ape in the jungle,

And tell them what do they think a bank is, anyhow, they
  had better go get the money from their wife's aunt
  or ungle.
But suppose people come in and they have a million and
  they want another million to pile on top of it,
Why, you brim with the milk of human kindness and you
  urge them to accept every drop of it.
And you lend them the million so then they have two
  million and this gives them the idea that they
  would be better off with four,
So they already have two million as security so you have
  no hesitation in lending them two more.
And all the vice-presidents nod their heads in rhythm,
And the only question asked is do the borrowers want the
  money sent or do they want to take it withm.
But please do not think that I am not fond of banks,
Because I think they deserve our appreciation and thanks.
Because they perform a valuable public service in
  elminating the jack-asses who go around saying
  that health and happiness are everything and money
  isn't essential,
Because as soon as they have to borrow some unimportant
  money to maintain their health and happiness they
  starve to death so they can't go around any more
  sneering at good old money, which is nothing short
  of providential.

Where Does the Money Go

CAROLYN HULL

The desk between us
is like a Texas desert.
The woman across from me,
like a scarf tied to a tree.

She is old, frayed, hard
to pin down. She doesn't remember
the names of things,
and she is crying.

I only need the loan till
my social security check comes in,
honey, she is saying as she sobs.
She smells unwashed, like she
is wearing her pajamas. Her face
folds and unfolds as she speaks.
I think I cashed my last check,
she goes on. If I did, I can't find
the money. I lost it. I'm hungry.

There are people outside my office
impatient for me to finish with this person
and get to them. Those people are real
loan customers, here to sign and get
their money. They can qualify. They are young
and know everything. This woman knows nothing,
not even that she was in my office
last month and we found her check,
crumpled in the vast cavern
bottom of her dark purse.

I ask her if we can look together.
She does not move. The wind has died.
The leaves of her memories fall
slowly downward toward the flat
geography of her life. She unclasps
the lock on the black purse and it opens,
full of dollar bills. They unfold and explode
onto the floor, her shoes, my office,
Ones, fives, tens, twenties.

What's this. I ask her, scooping and stuffing back.
She says, I don't remember.

The people who qualify are talking in loud voices.
Yes. I see them. I'm hurrying. Yes, this is a nuisance.

The old woman is smiling down at me.
Oh, honey, you found it. All my money.
I walk her out to the lobby.
Wait here for me. Wait until I can take you home.
She sits stiffly in the armchair.
She is forgetting. She is getting lost again.
I'm hungry, she says.
I know. I'll take you to lunch. Then home.
She is like a child.
She is my customer.

Declining the Loan

CAROLYN HULL

The light in the office is strong
enough only to question
the path through the numbers
that accompany this loan request.

I have sat here nearly an hour,
pencil wearing down and down
into the soft sponge of spread sheets
and flower fields of yellow legal pads.

It is like following bread crumbs
into the dark forest where trees are the stumps
of nines and sevens: the stained glass of light
through the leaves as seen in zeros and eights.
Slowly I have discovered a life: house payments,
car payments, credit cards, insurance, tax
returns, miscellaneous truths that stutter
when I ask, how are you going to pay this back?

Is the truth a desperate traveler who never comes to stay.
From his satchel, does truth extract the knife
that later draws blood.

I sense as I question the man that he aches
for that knife. It would be an easier honor
than hearing me say: there are several items
on your credit, your debt to income ratio
is too high. He looks at me as if I speak
a foreign language.

Does that mean I don't get it, he asks.
I'm afraid so, I say. I look directly at him,
protected by the authority of position,
the mythology of bankers.

He deflates as if that knife made an opening
and all the air escaped. He crumples into his clothes.
What am I going to do, his last question.
This truth and mine are dark strangers.
I don't want to talk to him about it anymore.

I want this to be a clean wound that will heal
with no scar. I don't watch him leave.
I go back to my work.

The numbers don't tell about the cold dinner,
left out for him because he's late.
They don't show the pain of pride to humility
as he shakes his head no when she asks about the money.
Those numbers have straight spines and still shoulders.
They shine like lasers.

And their light is only bright
enough to see the knife
dropped to the floor.
The handle in the shape of a six.

Variation on a Theme by Newbolt

JOHN BETJEMAN

The City will see him no more at important meetings
  In Renaissance board rooms by Edwin Cooper designed;
In his numerous clubs the politely jocular greetings
  Will be rather more solemn to-day with his death in mind.

Half mast from a first floor window, the Company's bunting
  Flops over Leadenhall Street in this wintry air
And his fellow directors, baulked of a good day's hunting
  Nod gloomily back to the gloomy commissionaire.

His death will be felt through the whole of the organization.
  In every branch of its vast managerial tree,
His brother-in-law we suppose will attend the cremation,
  A service will later be held in St. Katherine Cree.

But what of his guns?—he was always a generous giver.
  (Oh yes, of course, we will each of us send a wreath),
His yacht? and his shoot? and his beautiful reach of river?
  And all the clubs in his locker at Walton Heath?

I do not know, for my mind sees one thing only,
  A luxurious bedroom looking on miles of fir
From a Surrey height where his widow sits silent and lonely
  For a man whose love seemed wholly given to her.

Isaac Meek
An Epitaph

JOHN MASEFIELD

Hook-nosed was I, loose-lipped: greed fixed its gaze
In my young eyes ere they knew brass from gold;
Doomed to the blazing market-place my days—
A sweated chafferer of the bought and sold.

Fawned on and spat at, flattered and decried—
One only thing men asked of me—my price.
I lived, detested; and deserted, died,
Scorned by the virtuous, and the jest of vice.
And now, behold, blest child of Christ, my worth;
Stoop close: I have inherited the earth!

The Mortgage

WILL M. CARLETON

We worked through spring and winter—through summer and
    through fall
But the mortgage worked the hardest and the steadiest of us all;
It worked on nights and Sundays—it worked each holiday—
It settled down among us, and it never went away.
Whatever we kept from it seemed a'most as bad as theft;
It watched us every minute, and it ruled us right and left.
The rust and blight were with us sometimes, and sometimes not;
The dark-browed, scowling mortgage was forever on the spot.
The weevil and the cutworm, they went as well as came;
The mortgage stayed forever, eating hearty all the same.
It nailed up every window—stood guard at ever door—
And happiness and sunshine made their homes with us no more.

Till with failing crops and sickness we got stalled upon the grade,
And there came a dark day on us when the interest wasn't paid;
And there came a sharp foreclosure, and I kind o' lost my hold.
And grew weary and discouraged, and the farm was cheaply sold.
The children left and scattered when they hardly yet were grown;
My wife she pined an' perished, an' I found myself alone.
What she died of was "a mystery," an' the doctors never knew;
But *I* knew she died of *mortgage*—just as well's I wanted to.

If to trace a hidden sorrow were within the doctors' art,
They'd ha' found a mortgage lying on that woman's broken heart.
Worm or beetle—drought or tempest—on a farmer's land may fall;
But for first-class ruination, trust a mortgage 'gainst them all.

from Lucile

EARL OF LYTTON

A FORTNIGHT ago a report about town
Made me most apprehensive. Alas and alas!
I at once wrote and warn'd you. Well, now let that pass.
A run on the Bank about five days ago
Confirm'd my forebodings too terribly, though.
I drove down to the City at once: found the door
Of the Bank closed: the Bank had stopp'd payment at four.
Warrant out for MacNab; but MacNab was abroad:
Gone—we cannot tell where. I endeavour'd to get
Information: have learn'd nothing certain as yet—
Not even the way that old Ridley was gone:
Or with those securities what he had done:
Or whether they had been already call'd out:
If they are not, their fate is, I fear, past a doubt.

from Playboy
Canto III

WILLIAM OXLEY

It is a commonplace wealth must be defended
Hence lawyers, accountants and the like
Those remarkable creatures who manage to devour
Most of what they promise to protect and secure—

For wherever there is wealth it is under attack
And whoever has wealth is likely to lose it.
Indeed wealth itself seeks ever to elude one:
The guarantor of security, the god Money,
Is remarkably careless of His own security.
So there is nothing in the world easier to lose—
Not health, not happiness, not life itself—
Nothing easier to get without than money.
A thing intangible yet dazzling is wealth:
Often come to by stealth, always lost by stealth.
It is darkly, invisibly threatened, ever at risk:
Yet most of all at risk not only from others—
For all the envious greedy glances given—
But from oneself . . . so Jason taught me.

Really England's

WILLIAM OXLEY

It was like walking on history
        that capital "c" City
when I was younger there,
        from God-loaded Paul's
to new-built Barbican and London Wall
        and windy Bankside where
grim warehouses rotted beside
the mud-clotted river; historical
        as ever ruined Rome.
        Despite the gripe of money
in the guts, the indifferent many,
        it was culture's home
still, where gentle Will, laughing Ben
Johannis Miltonis and the best of men
        had snatched from the hands
        of hardline Time
the soul that's really England's—
        i.e., reader, yours and mine.

Underground Press (1956 Edition)

CHARLES BLACKBURN OWEN

He is something in the City
And, as if that were a pity,
The suit he wears is sombre black or grey,
With his tribe he is daily bound
For the nearest Underground,
But he stops to buy the Pink Un on the way.

By the brolly tightly furled,
The bowler slightly curled,
You may recognise the species at a glance
As they hurry down that hole
Like a scuttle-full of coal
With the typists (who come up in Petty France).

For the girls it should be fun,
Outnumbered four to one,
Yet City chaps will tell you (man to man),
Look, we are not above a caper
But there's pages of this paper
And we are packed like chipolatas in a can.

A bank has just gone bust,
There is another unit trust
And comment on the dollar premium rate,
A girl has more—or less,
She may need a larger dress,
But a City Man has got to concentrate.

City Leak

CHARLES BLACKBURN OWEN

The City Man delays to bid adieu
To what I should not miss (and nor would you);
He stands, reflective, hand upon the chain,
No loss, he ponders, but has matching gain,
What passes in this House and ebbs outside
Might float a trading empire on the tide.
Somewhere, could he but trace the business through,
A share that stands at one might go to two.

Golden Mean

CHARLES BLACKBURN OWEN

Old age is comforted by coin,
Youth by love's excesses;
O grant us Lord some middle date
When natural laws equivocate
And cash compounds with kisses.

The Bankers

BERTIE RAMSBOTTOM

Oh to be in banking
Now that April's here!
And celebrate a spanking,
Profitable year!
Some prefer to hear a
Cuckoo on the wing,

But oh to be a Clearer
Now that it is Spring!

Better than the crocus
Peeping through the soil;
Richer than the hocus
Pocus with the oil;
Money is the medium
Surer than the rest,
For sweetening the tedium
With the interest!

Other men may hanker
For a bluer sky,
But oh to be a banker
Now the rates are high!
It's freezing, more's the pity,
The darling buds of May,
But down in Dollar City,
It's roses all the way!

Cool it in Manhattan,
Keep it dark in Sioux,
Lest the profit pattern
Rouse the Revenue!
Tell 'em it's for gearing,
A little more to lend
But mainly it's for cheering
Up the dividend!

Oh to be in lending,
Joy for us and you;
When every buck we're spending
Spawns another two!
Loans are what we're here for,
Helping you invest,
Knowing you'll be back for more
To pay the interest!

Oh to be in Credit
As the seasons turn,
With other people's debit,
Filling up the urn!
Never mind the weather,
Banking is the thing;
As long as we're together,
It's everlasting Spring!

A Country Vicar at the Shrine of Mammon

SIR NICHOLAS GOODISON

"Wire bars advance in spirited trading"
—*Times*, November 1, 1966

My dear, I went to town today
To see to our affairs.
I called on George, who was away
But found a man who was pleased to say
He dealt in stocks and shares.

He spoke with confidence and wore
An Old St. Cuthbert's tie.
He knew the latest Test Match score
—416 for 4—
"A splendid start" said I.

He talked of economies world-wide.
He seemed by no means dim.
Theologically he was on our side
Which quickly led me to decide
I could confide in him.

I said that we—but I meant I—
Were sadly short of cash.
The cure, said he, would be to buy

Some three-month options on ICI
Which didn't sound too rash.

I did, and with an assuring grin
He leaned back in his chair.
"Of course" he went on, "lead and tin
Are the best investments to be in,
They'll double in a year."

This seemed so obviously true
That straightaway we paced
To a nearby office in EC2
Where he introduced a dealer who,
With philanthropic haste,

Sold me some lead, two tons of zinc,
Some wire bars, tin and grain
Jute, sugar, copra and (I think)
Some cocoa which he thought might sink
But must go up again.

In short, I fear I lost my head,
And had a spirited day.
Which means that we are in the red.
Wherefore, before we go to bed,
My dear one, let us pray.

Bankrupt

PATRICK TAYLOR

The day come-uppance came to Henry Lunceford-Price,
Lucinda, Babs and Nigel in the leafy street,
Another sign "for sale" went up; a small advice,
Went in the local paper, quiet and discreet,
To say "An auction will be held at Dunedin,
Of the house and all the personal effects therein."

A baby grand in mirror-white
Is gleaming by a bijou bar,
White sheepskin rugs are scattered on the floor
Six crates of claret make a dismal sight
Unopened in the hall, a car
Stands by the DIY iroko door

A Porsche—who'll bid for that?
Two horsey looking girls seem keen
To bid for pony tackle on the gate;
The bidding starts—"What offers for this hat
By Gucci? Twenty pounds—fifteen?"
A smile, a shrug, the gavel bangs for eight.

A cabinet with Lladro nuns
And figurines, two painted stone
Madonnas picked up carelessly in Rome,
A wall of imitation ancient guns
And prints. The auctioneer's drone
Goes on "And now this fine impressive home...."

With trinkets ticked in catalogues
Fur coats inspected on a rail
The patent shoes all rummaged through on racks,
We ruminate on life gone to the dogs—
A sordid Cinderella tale,
The forlorn pumpkin stopped dead in its tracks.

Running Porsches runs up bills
Good claret costs a bomb these days;
(They hadn't time to drink those final six
Unopened crates). It's fine to have ten tills;
Ten companies, when each one pays
The other's bills, but all these shady tricks
And oozing charm are not enough
When banks cut off the ready stuff.

And Henry, Lucy, Nige and Babs?
They stayed in Spain; Henry survives
With one small firm that's registered abroad,
He drives their van delivering kebabs
And propping up their louche and lazy lives
Or lies on beaches, brown and bored.

Canto III

Markets

Grace is given of God, but knowledge is
    bought in the market. . . .
            —Arthur Hugh Clough

Everyone lives by selling something.
            —Robert Louis Stevenson

The codfish lays ten thousand eggs,
The homely hen lays one.
The codfish never cackles
To tell you what she's done.
And so we scorn the codfish,
While the humble hen we prize.
Which only goes to show you
That it pays to advertise.
            —Anonymous

A California Ad Man Celebrates His Art

DAVID ALPAUGH

For those of you
who come here
out of spite
expecting to hear
a con man apologize—
prepare to gnash your teeth.

I am here to celebrate
the TV commercial—
the authentic poetry of our time:
lovingly produced,
widely received,
technically dazzling—
It really changes lives.

My title? "Tubular Poetics."

We deal in time and space:
thirty seconds of sound and light
rolling from earth to sky,
sky to earth,
kitchen to bedroom.

Our spirit is democratic.
We have made a pact
with Walt Whitman
to celebrate fecund America,
embracing all creeds, all colors:
men and women, young and old.

We praise hearth and home
in a manner that Beowulf
would understand.

Our art is tribal, mnemonic . . .
designed to be sung into the heart
by families gathered round the fire—

not warehoused in a public library
or read in private on a printed page.

Our words are deeds.
Like iron weapons
warriors carry into battle
to brandish at the foe
they must contribute to the victory.
If they don't sell cars or condoms
Grendel comes out of the fen
people lose food, status, power—
and like a singer of unwanted songs
under the castle wall
we are not allowed to get on the elevator
and rise to the thirty-eighth floor.

Like Bert Brecht, we believe that art
is an instrument for social progress.
We are concerned about the sick,
the homeless, those denied justice.
Much of our best work is in praise
of cold tablets, real estate chains
and motorcycle lawyers—
and every afternoon when school lets out
we suffer the little children to come unto us.

Like all great craftsmen
we find the material reality imposes
only partly to our purpose.
Our task is to build a world elsewhere,
with porcelain teeth, perfect complexions,
fully rounded bosoms and bottoms:
a pastoral living room . . .
an electronic bower of bliss . . .
zits, dandruff, athlete's foot,
bras that sag or ride up,
bad breath, fatal to love—
relentless fiends called
"Ring Around the Collar,"

"Hemorrhoidal Tissue,"
and surly appliances
that snap, snarl
and refuse to work.

In the cataclysms that ensue
we let good have its way with evil,
demonstrating the wisdom
shown a hundred times each day
by our hero with a thousand faces,
The Consumer.

Finally, like Milton
we have the highest moral purpose,
calling upon our Muse to justify
the ways of any product our agency assigns
to whatever target market is specified.

In doing so we've stumbled on free will
and with it a whole new tragic vision:
the knowledge that despite triumphal odes,
hymns, eclogues, paeans, songs of love,
and Juvenalian satire at its bitterest—
millions ignore the good and choose Brand X
dropping down to darkness and perdition.

These are just a few of the qualities
that link us to The Great Tradition.

Dobrodeyev

JIM LINDOP

I had met him but the once—
a sere and crackling Muscovite
who oddly reeked of Bovril
and would smoke cheap Boyards
which had stained his adder teeth
to match their brusk maize paper.

A black-edged card came
stapled to some invoices
and A4 sets of Ocean Bills of Lading
and it said
"With deep regret we must announce
the death of Dobrodeyev, Gregori,
in Moscow."
and to it stuck
but by the way
"Please pay
your overdue account."

Business Lunch

JIM LINDOP

A man came, round and shiny,
and busy-eyed.
He came, he said, to discuss
business,
set up lines of credit—
as it were.
He bragged, over a claret,
that he had
single-handedly shot
three hundred
brace of pheasant,
and many
smaller articles of game.
I made plain,
in strictest confidence,
my theory
that Hitler had been History's most
misjudged man.

Advertising Elegiacs

GAVIN EWART

Advertising! The men at the front are most terribly
    turdlike!
Backroom boys are the best; they can be human (a bit).
Clients are worst of the lot, bullies and thick as
    a blanket.
Presentations to *them* are true purgatorial things.
Ad-managers (if they're new) want to show you that
    they are the masters.
Chlorophyll once was the vogue: but the
    Chairman's wife didn't like green!
Everything greenside was out—so campaigns went
    out of the window.
Thinking up replacement crap, that was the
    terrible bore.
That's one example, of course, but examples of this
    come in thousands.
This is what drives them to drink, and the heart
    attack bang! at the end.
Suppose you've done it all once. Twice is not good.
    But a third time!
Three campaigns in a row, and the brain gets a bit
    of a twist!
Is there a moral at all? Is there, somewhere,
    consolation?
Only that death, in the end, bonks the nasties as
    well as the nice!

Happiness Is Girl-Shaped
(The Copywriter Sings)

GAVIN EWART

You're twice as trad as Acker Bilk,
you'd be delicious
                    crumbled into milk,
there is no other of your ilk!

You're very clearly bran-enriched
I'd like to have you
                    hedged and ditched,
no hype for you is over-pitched!

My heart, for you, has raced like Arkle
you've got that cute
                    refreshing sparkle,
you are my light that will not darkle!

You have that tangy lemon zest,
great things have happened
                    on your chest,
you're way out there beyond the rest!

You make life bright and dazzling new,
you are the first
                    of precious few,
I'd like to have a private view!

You set me off like fire alarms,
persuasive as
                    a salesman's charms,
I'd make down payments on your arms!

You are the rhyme that's always true,
the whitest wash
                    that's slightly blue—
let me consume my life with you!

The Caged Copywriter

GAVIN EWART

"Office life, investment, interest rates, corporate politics, annual reports—these are not subjects which would seem especially congenial to poetry."
—Dana Gioia. *The Hudson Review*

I sat alone in so many small rooms
behind glass partitions,
or open plan with others,
and wrestled all day with the headlines,
with the hundreds of words of copy,
biro and two-finger-tapping
on the beaten-up old typewriter. . . .

I sat in on so many meetings
where they told us the Unique Sales Proposition
and listed the Sales Points:
it's blue, it's chemically neutral, it's waterproof.
And the boys from Research narrowed down the copy
to the angelic head of a pin.

Requisitions, work demanded, campaigns with posters—
all filtered through a Copy Chief or Creative Director,
typists making nonsense of the carefullest copy
(the clever writers wooed them into clean Top Copies).

After the liquid lunches the authoritarians were mellow . . .

And this went on for days and weeks and years,
tedium tempered by occasional entertainment,
the good expensive food wilted in the face of the clients
(the talk was of cars, they never read a book,
just once somebody mentioned Dornford Yates with approval),
you couldn't get drunk because of The Image.
It was, virtually, a Tantalus Situation.

The clients bullied the agencies, the Account Executives
bullied the Creative Departments—
they had Brigade of Guards ties and friends in the City.
Money may be "a kind of poetry." It certainly talks.
From the Fifties to the Seventies I heard it talking.

We were pedestrians on the plains of the working week,
the expendable infantry below the peaks of Success.
Who wants to read about a routine?
No love affairs, no murders, no adventures.
Just the summer lightning of a sparkling campaign.
Just a lot of figures, a lot of sums of money.

In a big store, does a shoe
ever write a poem about the Carpet Department?

from Omar Khayyam

EDWARD FITZGERALD

Indeed the Idols I have loved so long
Have done my Credit in Men's Eye much wrong!
Have drown'd my Honour in a shallow Cup,
And sold my Reputation for a Song.

. . . .

And much as Wine has play'd the Infidel,
And robb'd me of my Robe of Honour—well,
I often wonder what the Vintners buy
One half so precious as the Goods they sell.

A Consumer's Report

PETER PORTER

The name of the product I tested is *Life*,
I have completed the form you sent me
and understand that my answers are confidential.

I had it as a gift,
I didn't feel much while using it,
in fact I think I'd have liked to be more excited.
It seemed gentle on the hands
but left an embarrassing deposit behind.
It was not economical
and I have used much more than I thought
(I suppose I have about half left
but it's difficult to tell)—
although the instructions are fairly large
there are so many of them
I don't know which to follow, especially
as they seem to contradict each other.
I'm not sure such a thing
should be put in the way of children—
It's difficult to think of a purpose
for it. One of my friends says
it's just to keep its maker in a job.
Also the price is much too high
Things are piling up so fast,
after all, the world got by
for a thousand million years
without this, do we need it now?
(Incidentally, please ask your man
to stop calling me "the respondent,"
I don't like the sound of it.)
There seems to be a lot of different labels,
sizes and colours should be uniform,
the shape is awkward, it's waterproof

but not heat resistant, it doesn't keep
yet it's very difficult to get rid of:
whenever they make it cheaper they seem
to put less in—if you say you don't
want it, then it's delivered anyway.
I'd agree it's a popular product,
it's got into the language; people
even say they're on the side of it.
Personally I think it's overdone,
a small thing people are ready
to behave badly about. I think
we should take it for granted. If its
experts are called philosophers or market
researchers or historians, we shouldn't
care. We are the consumers and the last
law makers. So finally, I'd buy it.
But the question of a "best buy"
I'd like to leave until I get
the competitive product you said you'd send.

After Martial: V. xviii

PETER PORTER

Comes December and the giving season, when
every shop is stocked with gadgets—hand-
kerchiefs with Aunt's initials, silly spoons
to lock away forever, candles sculptured
like ten castles, personalized mauve paper
with embossed addresses, and amazing plums
that only Fortnum's would import: why have I
sent nothing better than my own new poems
(home-made nourishment indeed)—am I
self-satisfied or merely stingy? My thoughts
aren't pendulums to swing back all my way—

Great gifts are guiles and look for gifts again;
My trifles come as treasures from my mind.
I quote. To catch the greedy bream you cast
the glittering fly. Which of us hasn't ex-
pectations of his benefactors as
his gods? In truth, the poor man. Quintianus,
is generous to his well-heeled friend when he
looks him out a keepsake, writes a card,
and leaves him off his Christmas Shopping List!

Shopping Scenes

PETER PORTER

1

Huge heads of amiable malice
Hang across the shop in processed air
Saying: "At Uncle Holly's Christmas Hollow, see Alice
Disembowel the Mad Hatter and the March Hare."

2

Behind his half-moon glasses, the
Sesquipedalian don is triumphant.
He's found an 1870 Book of Nursery Care—
The same stiff-backed volume on his bare
Backside wielded by his arthritic aunt
Terrified his childhood. Terror warmly
Returns. 3/6 will set him free again—
Happy Return of guilt and certainty and pain.

3

Snubbed by that bouffant giggly girl,
All tit and bum drinking Babycham
At the office party, he leaves early
And dashes into the record shop, buys
"La Favorita" with his Christmas bonus.
Spending money is the kindest orgasm.

4

(An advertising man in the Palermo Catacombs)

Panthering here on handsewn turquoise suede.
He captions this Capuchin light and shade.

This Memento Mori floods Harper's Bazaar.
That "overwhelming minority" of readers stares

At the mummies' now exclusive dust.
The season's silhouette, the witty bust.

The mask white model has a little heat.
Mr. Avedon makes death famous. "The feet

In off-the-shoulder shoes are real breath-
takers." It's the way out here at the House of Death.

We Would Refer You to Our Service Department, If We Had One

OGDEN NASH

It fills me with elation
To live in such a mechanical-minded nation,
Surrounded not only by the finest scenery
But also the most machinery,
Where every prospect is attractive
And people are radioactive,
Reading books with show-how
Written by scientists with know-how.
Breathes there with soul so dead a fossil
Who never to himself hath said, Production is colossal?
Obviously civilization is far from a crisis
When the land teems with skilled craftsmen skillfully
        manufacturing gadgets and mechanical devices.
Millions of washing machines and electric refrigerators.
Are shipped from the shipping rooms of their originators.

Streamlined dreamlined automobiles roll off the assembly
   lines in battalions and droves.
Millions of radios pour from the factories for house-
   wives to listen to in the time they save through
   not having to slice their pre-sliced loaves.
So when everybody has a houseful and a garageful of
   mechanical perfection no one has any worries, but
   if you want a worry, I will share one.
Which is, Why is it that when seemingly anybody can
   make an automobile or a washing machine, nobody
   can repair one?
If you want a refrigerator or an automatic can opener
   or a razor that plays "Begin the Beguine" you can
   choose between an old rose or lavender or blue
   one.
But after you've got it, why if anything goes wrong
   don't think you'll find anybody to fix it, just throw
   it away and buy a new one.
Oh well, anyhow here I am nearly forty-five,
And still alive.

Song against Grocers

G. K. CHESTERTON

God made the wicked Grocer
   For a mystery and a sign
That men might shun the awful shops
   And go to inns to dine.

He keeps a lady in a cage
   Most cruelly all day,
And makes her count and calls her "Miss"
   Until she fades away.

He crams with cans of poisoned meat
    The subjects of the King
And when they die by thousands
    Why, he laughs like anything.

The righteous minds of innkeepers
    Induce them now and then
To crack a bottle with a friend
    Or treat unmoneyed men.

a salesman is an it that stinks Excuse

E. E. CUMMINGS

a salesman is an it that stinks Excuse

Me whether it's president of the you were say
or a jennelman name misder finger isn't
important whether it's millions of other punks
or just a handful absolutely doesn't
matter and whether it's in lonjewray

or shrouds is immaterial it stinks

a salesman is an it that stinks to please

but whether to please itself or someone else
makes no more difference than if it sells
hate condoms education snakeoil vac
uumcleaners terror strawberries democ
ra(caveat emptor)cy superfluous hair

or Think We've Met subhuman rights Before

from The Gods of the Copybook Headings

RUDYARD KIPLING

As I pass through my incarnations in every age and race,
I make my proper prostrations to the Gods of the Market-Place.
Peering through reverent fingers I watch them flourish and fall,
And the Gods of the Copybook Headings, I notice, outlast
    them all.

We were living in trees when they met us. They showed us each
    in turn
That Water would certainly wet us, as Fire would certainly burn;
But we found them lacking in Uplift, Vision and Breadth of Mind,
So we left them to teach the Gorillas while we followed the March
    of Mankind.

We moved as the Spirit listed. *They* never altered their pace,
Being neither cloud nor wind-borne like the Gods of the
    Market-Place;
But they always caught up with our progress, and presently word
    would come
That a tribe had been wiped off its icefield, or the lights had gone
    out in Rome.

     . . . .

In the Carboniferous Epoch we were promised abundance for all,
By robbing selected Peter to pay for collective Paul;
But, though we had plenty of money, there was nothing our
    money could buy,
And the Gods of the Copybook Headings said: "*If you don't
    work you die.*"

Then the Gods of the Market tumbled, and their smooth-tongued
    wizards withdrew,
And the hearts of the meanest were humbled and began to believe
    it was true

That All is not Gold that Glitters, and Two and Two make Four—
And the Gods of the Copybook Headings limped up to explain it
   once more.

.   .   .   .

As it will be in the future, it was at the birth of Man—
There are only four things certain since Social Progress began:
That the Dog returns to his Vomit and the Sow returns to
   her Mire,
And the burnt Fool's bandaged finger goes wabbling back to
   the Fire;

And that after this is accomplished, and the brave new world
   begins
When all men are paid for existing and no man must pay for
   his sins,
As surely as Water will wet us, as surely as Fire will burn,
The Gods of the Copybook Headings with terror and slaughter
   return!

Canto IV

It's no go my honey love,
     it's no go my poppet:
Work your hands from day to day,
     the winds will blow the profit.
          —Louis Macneice, *A Classical Education*

Who first invented Work—and tied the free
And holy-day rejoicing spirit down
To the ever-haunting importunity
Of business, in the green fields, and the towns—
To plough-loom-anvil-spade-and, oh, most sad,
To this dry drudgery of the desk's dead wood?
          —Charles Lamb, *Letter to Barton*

What to Know about Hanging On

JAMES A. AUTRY

I
Why do they keep on working,
the ones who should take everything,
the disability time,
the vacation,
the wink-and-look-the-other-way extras
they could get at a time like this?
Why don't they head for the fishing hole
they always talked about,
or the mountains,
or that spot far away from the cold,
the one they promised to send pictures
for us to hang in the garage
above our snow shovels?
Why do they make up excuses
to come in on time every morning
and return phone calls
and answer correspondence
and talk about next year's sales goals
and the plan
and the earnings
and the stock price
and the chances of a takeover—
everything as ordinary as always?

II
We used to say,
as they did,
if it happened to us
we would kiss the job good-bye

and pack every remaining minute
with people we love
and things we love to do.
Through all those years
it did not occur to us
that what we really love to do
is the work—
never mind the job
with all its trappings,
those things we have to do
so we can do the work,
and never mind that we talked about
loving the company
when we really meant
loving the people.

But now, watching someone hang on,
I long to say the words we feel
but never say,
about how hard it is to show
the love of what we do together,
until we face the certainty
that it is about to end.

Toads

PHILIP LARKIN

Why should I let the toad *work*
    Squat on my life?
Can't I use my wit as a pitchfork
    And drive the brute off?

Six days of the week it soils
 With its sickening poison—
Just for paying a few bills!
 That's out of proportion.

Lots of folk live on their wits:
 Lecturers, lispers,
Losels, loblolly-men, louts—
 They don't end as paupers;

Lots of folk live up lanes
 With fires in a bucket,
Eat windfalls and tinned sardines—
 They seem to like it.

Their nippers have got bare feet,
 Their unspeakable wives
Are skinny as whippets—and yet
 No one actually *starves*.

Ah, were I courageous enough
 To shout *Stuff your pension!*
But I know, all too well, that's the stuff
 That dreams are made on:

For something sufficiently toad-like
 Squats in me, too;
Its hunkers are heavy as hard luck,
 And cold as snow,

And will never allow me to blarney
 My way to getting
The fame and the girl and the money
 All at one sitting.

I don't say, one bodies the other
 One's spiritual truth;
But I do say it's hard to lose either,
 When you have both.

The Managers

W. H. AUDEN

In the bad old days it was not so bad:
    The top of the ladder
Was an amusing place to sit; success
    Meant quite a lot—leisure
And huge meals, more palaces filled with more
    Objects, books, girls, horses
Than one would ever get round to, and to be
    Carried uphill while seeing
Others walk. To rule was a pleasure when
    One wrote a death-sentence
On the back of the Ace of Spades and played on
    With a new deck. Honours
Are not so physical or jolly now,
    For the species of Powers
We are used to are not like that. Could one of them
    Be said to resemble
The Tragic Hero, the Platonic Saint,
    Or would any painter
Portray one rising triumphant from a lake
    On a dolphin, naked,
Protected by an umbrella of cherubs? Can
    They so much as manage
To behave like genuine Caesars when alone
    Or drinking with cronies,
To let their hair down and be frank about
    The world? It is doubtful.
The last word on how we may live or die
    Rests today with such quiet
Men, working too hard in rooms that are too big,
    Reducing to figures
What is the matter, what is to be done.
    A neat little luncheon

Of sandwiches is brought to each on a tray,
    Nourishment they are able
To take with one hand without looking up
    From papers a couple
Of secretaries are needed to file,
    From problems no smiling
Can dismiss. The typewriters never stop
    But whirr like grasshoppers
In the silent siesta heat as, frivolous
    Across their discussions,
From woods unaltered by our wars and our vows
    There drift the scents of flowers
And the songs of birds who will never vote
    Or bother to notice
Those distinguishing marks a lover sees
    By instinct and policemen
Can be trained to observe. Far into the night
    Their windows burn brightly
And, behind their backs bent over some report,
    On every quarter,
For ever like a god or a disease
    There on the earth the reason
In all its aspects why they are tired, the weak,
    The inattentive, seeking
Someone to blame. If, to recuperate
    They go a-playing, their greatness
Encounters the bow of the chef or the glance
    Of the ballet-dancer
Who cannot be ruined by any master's fall.
    To rule must be a calling,
It seems, like surgery or sculpture; the fun
    Neither love nor money
But taking necessary risks, the test
    Of one's skill, the question,
If difficult, their own reward. But then
    Perhaps one should mention

Also what must be a comfort as they guess
　　In times like the present
When guesses can prove so fatally wrong
　　The fact of belonging
To the very select indeed, to those
　　For whom, just supposing
They do, there will be places on the last
　　Plane out of disaster.
No; no one is really sorry for their
　　Heavy gait and careworn
Look, nor would they thank you if you said you were.

Executive

JOHN BETJEMAN

I am a young executive. No cuffs than mine are cleaner;
I have a Slimline brief-case and I use the firm's Cortina,
In every roadside hostelry from here to Burgess Hill
The *maitres d'hotel* all know me well and let me sign the bill.

You ask me what it is I do. Well actually, you know,
I'm partly a liaison man and partly P.R.O.
Essentially I integrate the current export drive
And basically I'm viable from ten o'clock till five.

For vital off-the-record work—that's talking transport-wise—
I've a scarlet Aston-Martin—and does she go? She flies!
Pedestrians and dogs and cats—we mark them down for slaughter.
I also own a speed-boat which has never touched the water.

She's built of fibre-glass, of course. I call her "Mandy Jane"
After a bird I used to know—No soda, please, just plain—
And how did I aquire her? Well to tell you about that
And to put you in the picture I must wear my other hat.

I do some mild developing. The sort of place I need
Is a quiet country market town that's rather run to seed.
A luncheon and a drink or two, a little *savoir faire*—
I fix the Planning Officer, the Town Clerk and the Mayor.

And if some preservationist attempts to interfere
A "dangerous structure" notice from the Borough Engineer
Will settle any buildings that are standing in our way—
The modern style, sir, with respect, has really come to stay.

The Stenographers

P. K. PAGE

After the brief bivouac of Sunday,
their eyes, in the forced march of Monday to Saturday,
hoist the white flag, flutter in the snow storm of paper,
haul it down and crack in the midsun of temper.

In the pause between the first draft and the carbon
they glimpse the smooth hours when they were children—
the ride in the ice-cart, the ice-man's name,
the end of the route and the long walk home;

remember the sea where floats at high tide
were sea marrows growing on the scatter-green vine
or spools of grey toffee, or wasps' nests on water;
remember the sand and the leaves of the country.

Bell rings and they go and the voice draws their pencil
like a sled across snow; when its runners are frozen
rope snaps and the voice then is pulling no burden
but runs like a dog on the winter of paper.

Their climates are winter and summer—no wind
for the kites of their hearts—no wind for a flight;
a breeze at the most, to tumble them over
and leave them like rubbish—the boy-friends of blood.

In the inch of the noon as they move they are stagnant.
The terrible calm of the noon is their anguish;
the lip of the counter, the shapes of the straws
like icicles breaking their tongues are invaders.

Their beds are their oceans—salt water of weeping
the waves that they know—the tide before sleep;
and fighting to drown they assemble their sheep
in columns and watch them leap desks for their fences
and stare at them with their own mirror-worn faces.

In the felt of the morning the calico minded,
sufficiently starched, insert papers, hit keys,
efficient and sure as their adding machines;
yet they weep in the vault, they are taut as net curtains
stretched upon frames. In their eyes I have seen
the pin men of madness in marathon trim
race round the track of the stadium pupil.

The Marunouchi Building

NAKAHARA CHUYA

Ah! lunch and
There goes the siren,
There goes the siren.
Out they stream,
Out they stream.

Salarymen out for lunch,
Aimlessly swinging arms.
And still out they stream,
Out they stream.

Vast building,
Coal-black tiny
Tiny exit.

Thin cloud filming the sky,
Thin cloud and
Dust blowing up.

Comical salarymen
Looking up,
Looking down.

Why should I be
The great man that
I know I am?

Ah! lunch and
There goes the siren,
There goes the siren.

Out they stream,
Out they stream.

Vast building,
Coal-black tiny
Tiny exit.

The siren mounts on the wind,
Echoes, re-echoes, and blows away.

Translated from the Japanese
by Geoffrey Bownas

What the Chairman Told Tom

BASIL BUNTING

POETRY? It's a hobby,
I run model trains.
Mr. Shaw there breeds pigeons.

It's not work. You don't sweat.
Nobody pays for it.
You *could* advertise soap.

Art, that's opera; or repertory—
The Desert Song.
Nancy was in the chorus.

But to ask for twelve pounds a week—
married, aren't you?—
you've got a nerve.

How could I look a bus conductor
in the face
if I paid you twelve pounds?

Who says it's poetry, anyhow?
My ten year old
can do it *and* rhyme.

I get three thousand and expenses,
a car, vouchers,
but I'm an accountant.

They do what I tell them,
my company.
What do *you* do?

Nasty little words, nasty long words,
it's unhealthy.
I want to wash when I meet a poet.

They're Reds, addicts,
all delinquents.
What you write is rot.

Mr. Hines says so, and he's a schoolteacher,
he ought to know,
Go and find *work*.

I Hear America Singing

WALT WHITMAN

I HEAR America singing, the varied carols I hear,
Those of mechanics, each one singing his as it should be blithe and
strong,
The carpenter singing his as he measures his plank or beam,
The mason singing his as he makes ready for work, or leaves off
work,
The boatman singing what belongs to him in his boat, the deck-
hand singing on the steamboat deck,
The shoemaker singing as he sits on his bench, the hatter singing
as he stands,

The wood-cutter's song, the ploughboy's on his way in the morn-
ing, or at noon intermission or at sundown,
The delicious singing of the mother, or of the young wife at work,
or of the girl sewing or washing,
Each singing what belongs to him or her and to none else,
The day what belongs to the day—at night the party of young
fellows, robust, friendly
Singing with open mouths their strong melodious songs.

From Thirty Bob a Week

JOHN DAVIDSON

I COULDN'T touch a stop and turn a screw,
  And set the blooming world a-work for me,
Like such as cut their teeth—I hope, like you—
  On the handle of a skeleton gold key;
I cut mine on a leek, which I eat it every week:
  I'm a clerk at thirty bob as you can see.

But I don't allow it's luck and all a toss;
    There's no such thing as being starred and crossed;
It's just the power of some to be a boss,
    And the bally power of others to be bossed:
I face the music, sir; you bet I ain't a cur;
    Strike me lucky if I don't believe I'm lost!

For like a mole I journey in the dark,
    A-travelling along the underground
From my Pillar'd Halls and broad Suburbean Park,
    To come the daily dull official round;
And home again at night with my pipe all alight,
    A-scheming how to count ten bob a pound.

And it's often very cold and very wet,
    And my missis stitches towels for a hunks;
And the Pillar'd Halls is half of it to let—
    Three rooms about the size of travelling trunks.
And we cough, my wife and I, to dislocate a sigh,
    When the noisy little kids are in their bunks.

But you never hear her do a growl or whine,
    For she's made of flint and roses, very odd;
And I've got to cut my meaning rather fine,
    Or I'd blubber, for I'm made of greens and sod:
So p'r'aps we are in Hell for all that I can tell,
    And lost and damn'd and served up hot to God.

.   .   .   .

They say it daily up and down the land
    And easy as you take a drink, it's true;
But the difficultest go to understand,
    And the difficultest job a man can do.
Is to come it brave and meek with thirty bob a week,
    And feel that that's the proper thing for you.

It's a naked child against a hungry wolf;
    It's playing bowls upon a splitting wreck;
It's walking on a string across a gulf
    With the millstones fore-and-aft about your neck;
But the thing is daily done by many and many a one;
    And we fall, face forward, fighting, on the deck.

Work

PUSHKIN

HERE is the long-bided hour: the labour of years is
    accomplished.
Why should this sadness unplumbed secretly weigh
    on my heart?
Is it, my work being done, I stand like a labourer,
    useless,
One who has taken his pay, a stranger to tasks that
    are new?
Is it the work I regret, the silent companion of mid-
    night,
Friend of the golden-haired Dawn, friend of the
    gods of the hearth?

Translated from the Russian
by Babette Deutsch and Avrahm Yarmolinski

The Ruined Maid

THOMAS HARDY

"O 'Melia, my dear, this does everything crown!
Who could have supposed I should meet you in Town?
And whence such fair garments, such prosperi-ty?"—
"O didn't you know I'd been ruined?" said she.

—"You left us in tatters, without shoes or socks,
Tired of digging potatoes, and spudding up docks;
And now you've gay bracelets and bright feathers three!"—
"Yes: that's how we dress when we're ruined," said she.

—"At home in the barton you said 'thee' and 'thou,'
And 'thik oon,' and 'theäs oon,' and 'r'other'; but now
Your talking quite fits 'ee for high compa-ny!"—
"A polish is gained with one's ruin," said she.

—"Your hands were like paws then, your face blue and bleak,
But now I'm bewitched by your delicate cheek,
And your little gloves fit as on any la-dy!"—
"We never do work when we're ruined," said she.

—"You used to call home-life a hag-ridden dream,
And you'd sigh, and you'd sock; but at present you seem
To know not of megrims or melancho-ly!"—
"True. One's pretty lively when ruined," said she.

—"I wish I had feathers, a fine sweeping gown,
And a delicate face, and could strut about Town!"—
"My dear—a raw country girl, such as you be,
Cannot quite expect that. You ain't ruined," said she.

Craftsmen

VITA SACKVILLE-WEST

ALL craftsmen share a knowledge. They have held
Reality down fluttering to a bench;
Cut wood to their own purposes; compelled
The growth of pattern with the patient shuttle;
Drained acres to a trench.
Control is theirs. They have ignored the subtle
Release of spirit from the jail of shape.
They have been concerned with prison, not escape;

Pinioned the fact, and let the rest go free,
And out of need made inadvertent art.
All things designed to play a faithful part
Build up their plain particular poetry.
Tools have their own integrity;

The sneath of scythe curves rightly to the hand,
The hammer knows its balance, knife its edge,
All tools inevitably planned,
Stout friends, with pledge
Of service; with their crotchets too
That masters understand,
And proper character, and separate heart,
But always to their chosen temper true.
—So language, smithied at the common fire,
Grew to its use; as sneath and shank and haft
Of well-grained wood, nice instruments of craft,
Curve to the simple mould the hands require,
Born of the needs of man.
The poet like the artisan
Works lonely with his tools; picks up each one,
Blunt mallet knowing, and the quick thin blade,
And plane that travels when the hewing's done;
Rejects, and chooses; scores a fresh faint line;
Sharpens, intent upon his chiselling;
Bends lower to examine his design,
If it be truly made,
And brings perfection to so slight a thing
But in the shadows of his working-place,
Dust-moted, dim,
Among the chips and lumber of his trade,
Lifts never his bowed head, a breathing-space
To look upon the world beyond the sill,
The world framed small, in distance, for to him
The world and all its weight are in his will.
As the poor joiner, working at his wood,

Knew not the tree from which the planks were taken,
Knew not the glade from which the trunk was brought,
Knew not the soil in which the roots were fast,
Nor by what centuries of gales the boughs were shaken,
But holds them all beneath his hands at last.

Dead Factory at Night

MICHAEL IVENS

Machines moulder.   In the moonlight
Sadly walk   ghosts of foremen.
Owls perch   on the machine shop;
Mice scuttle   in the foundry.

Eager boys   started on capstans;
Lip-sticked girls   acquired type-writers.
Fox-trots   at canteen dances
Brought love   and many children.

No more   eager salesmen
Hand in   steady orders.
Dust gathers   on fading time-cards.
In the yard   walk ghosts of foremen.

Lankro Chemicals

R. JOYNSON

At length they brought me to this place,
Smothered in a gloom of light.
A steel-clad bower,
Lofty without space,
Enclosed yet crawling with chill winds.

From the floors, walls, pounding organs of this erection
Sweat forth the ceaseless steams,
The fetid fumes.
Pavonine plumes
Etch my lungs and eyes.

My stare, scraping, sweeps an arterial web of iron-wrought forms,
Mystic, elusive, from some Satanic hand.
Blue, bent drones skulkly go,
To and fro, to and fro,
Amid this steaming, steely forest.

. . . Of the Forge and Foundry at the Austin Motor Company, Longbridge 1932–39

JOHN MARSH

In the momentary halo of a Forge's drop
I see the rivers of human sweat
Coursing down the foreheads and facial crevices
Of fearful men.
In the Foundry's sickly air,
Brown darkened and stygian fumes
Penetrate the souls of men who struggle to be gentle.
Ever the wild harlotry of machines
Relentless movements by conveyors
Up and over achieving encycling tasks
Planned by humane geniuses in offices.
Skills of shopfloor craftsmen.
Dissolve slowly to disappear
In the jungle undergrowth of mechanisation.

Men perish here, inevitably,
In the sure and seeping death of pride.

Selling Myself

JOHN MARSH

I arrive at the gate; after waiting they speak to me.
They say I have little skill—
I am not worthy of what I ask—
Others are waiting; so, fearful of going away empty
I bargain and accept a lesser rate than that for which I'd hoped.
A new world enfolds me
Reluctantly at first;
Strange men speak at me
New tools and disciplines, methods
Sap my freedom
And interest.
Friday comes and payment
Compensates for much
I feared.
Though self respect
Returns a little now and then
As I buy
A piece of affluence
In life's bargain basement
Where I live.

The Miner's Helmet

GEORGE MACBETH

My father wore it working coal at Shotts
When I was one. My mother stirred his broth
And rocked my cradle with her shivering hands
While this black helmet's long-lost miner's lamp

Showed him the road home. Through miles of coal
His fragile skull, filled even then with pit-props,
Lay in a shell, the brain's blue-printed future
Warm in its womb. From sheaves of saved brown paper,
Baring an oval into weeks of dust.
I pull it down: its laced straps move to admit
My larger brows; like an abdicated king's
Gold crown of thirty years ago, I touch it
With royal fingers, feel its image firm—
Hands grown to king's hands calloused on the pick,
Feet slow like king's feet on the throneward gradient
Up to the coal-face—but the image blurs
Before it settles: there were no crusades.
My father died a draughtsman, drawing plans
In an airy well-lit office above the ground
Beneath which his usurpers, other kings,
Reigned by the fallen helmet he resigned
Which I inherit as a concrete husk.
I hand it back to gather dust on the shelf.

from Biography

JOHN MASEFIELD

OTHER bright days of action have seemed great;
Wild days in a pampero off the Plate;
Good swimming days, at Hog Back or the Coves
Which the young gannet and the corbie loves;
Surf-swimming between rollers, catching breath
Between the advancing grave and breaking death,
Then shooting up into the sunbright smooth
To watch the advancing roller bare her tooth,
And days of labour also, loading, hauling;
Long days at winch or capstan, heaving, pawling;
The days with oxen, dragging stones from blasting,

And dusty days in mills, and hot days masting.
Trucking on dust-dry deckings smooth like ice,
And hunts in mighty wool-racks after mice;
Mornings with buckwheat when the fields did blanch
With White Leghorns come from the chicken ranch.

.   .   .   .

This many pictured world of many passions
Wears out the nations as a woman fashions,
And what life is is much to very few,
Men being so strange, so mad, and what men do
So good to watch or share; but when men count
Those hours of life that were a bursting fount,
Sparkling the dusty heart with living springs,
There seems a world, beyond our earthly things,
Gated by golden moments, each bright time
Opening to show the city white like lime,
High-towered and many-peopled. This made sure,
Work that obscures those moments seems impure,
Making our not-returning time of breath
Dull with the ritual and records of death,
That frost of fact by which our wisdom gives
Correctly stated death to all that lives.

Best trust the happy moments. What they gave
Makes man less fearful of the certain grave.
And gives his work compassion and new eyes,
The days that make us happy make us wise.

The Job Description

BERTIE RAMSBOTTOM

I trod, where fools alone may tread,
Who speak what's better left unsaid,
The day I asked the boss his view
On what I was supposed to do;

For, after two years in the task,
I thought it only right to ask,
In case I'd got it badly wrong
Ad-hoc'ing as I went along.

He raised his desultory eyes
And made no effort to disguise
That, what had caused my sudden whim,
Had equally occurred to him;
And thus did we embark upon
Our classic corporate contretemps,
To separate the fact from fiction,
Bedeviling my job description.

For first he asked me to construe
A list of things I really do;
While he—he promised—would prepare
A note of what he thought they were;
And, with the two, we'd take as well
The expert view from Personnel,
And thus eliminate the doubt
On what my job was all about.

But when the boss and I conflated
The tasks we'd separately stated,
The evidence became abundant
That one of us must be redundant;
For what I stated I was doing
He claimed himself to be pursuing,
While my role, on his definition,
Was way outside my recognition.

He called in Personnel to give
A somewhat more definitive
Reply, but they, by way of answer,
Produced some vague extravaganza,
Depicting, in a web of charts,
Descriptive and prescriptive parts

Of tasks, the boss and I agree,
Can't possibly refer to me.

So, hanging limply as I am,
In limbo on the diagram,
Suspended by a dotted line
From functions that I thought were mine,
I feel it's maybe for the best
I made my innocent request;
I hopefully await their view
On which job of the three to do!

Canto V

Corporate Life

A man who has no office to go to—
I don't care who he is—
is a trial of which you can have no conception. . . .
          —George Bernard Shaw, *The Irrational Knot*

This is the world in which he lives:
Four walls, a desk, a swivel chair,
A doorway with no door to close,
Vents to bring in air.
          —Dana Gioia, *The Man in the Open Doorway*

I Have Arrived

NATASHA JOSEFOWITZ

I have not seen the plays in town
    only the computer printouts
I have not read the latest books
    only The Wall Street Journal
I have not heard the birds sing this year
    only the ringing of phones
I have not taken a walk anywhere
    but from the parking lot to my office
I have not shared a feeling in years
    but my thoughts are known to all
I have not listened to my own needs
    but what I want I get
I have not shed a tear in ages
    I have arrived
Is this where I was going?

The Executive's Wife

NATASHA JOSEFOWITZ

Company for dinner...
his business associates,
hors d'oeuvres,
hot and cold.
Be sure to have
enough liquor in the house,
enough soda,
dress attractively,

but not too.
House should be clean,
children out of the way.
Greet them smiling,
chitchat.
Don't talk business.
If they do,
they'll apologise
for being boring.
"I don't mind—
in fact I'm interested."
Polite smiles,
nice home,
lovely dinner,
well brought-up children,
becoming dress,
charming wife.
Oh, thank you,
thank you for your favorable comments
on the house,
    the dinner,
    the children,
    the dress,
    the wife
(in that order?)
It was a huge success!

So why did the charming wife
    in her becoming dress
    with the well brought-up children
    and the lovely dinner
    in the nice home . . .
    Leave?

for RJM

QUENTIN DE LA BEDOYERE

The boardroom table with its glossy sheen
Reflects the faces in its surface seen,
And twisted features mirrored in its view
Distort distorted images anew.
They gape and snatch like fish before the bait
And dart at problems no one cares to state.
The hobby-horsers spray their Xeroxed sheet;
The slide projector hums with idle heat;
The flip chart shudders as its pages fly;
The marker pens, like brains, are running dry.
Each fence of stripes which palisades each shirt
Conceals a cause the meeting to subvert—
But several causes thrusting several ways
Make progress like a blind man through a maze.
Our democratic chairman takes no sides;
He yields his place, and Anarchy presides.

Earl's Office

JIM LINDOP

Earl's desk is foursquare oak, masculine as whiskey.
The walls are bare, but for a vista of blue hills
scarred by a barbed-wire fence and good ole country road,
and, oh, his Cleartype ColorLamolex framed map
—counties, states and clapboard downhome U.S. townships.
Earl's jacket hangs from a stand like a joshua tree,
and matching colonial brass desk lamps flutter moths,
whose dying shades play grand guignol on Earl's brown walls.

Earl's telephones are ranged like field artillery.
His swivel chair encompasses a view of trees
zipping up the distance out beyond the gray glass
guillotined by louvre blinds like calaboose bars.

The Man in the Open Doorway

DANA GIOIA

This is the world in which he lives:
Four walls, a desk, a swivel chair,
A doorway with no door to close,
Vents to bring in air.

There are two well-marked calendars,
Some pencils, and a telephone
The women at the front desk answer
Leaving him alone.

There is a clock he hardly sees
Beside the window on the wall.
It moves in only one direction,
Never stops at all.

Outside the February wind
Scrapes up against the windowpane,
And a blue-green land is fading,
Scarred by streaks of rain.

The phones go off. The files are locked.
But the doorway still is lit at night
Like the tall window of a church
Bleached in winter light.

Sometimes the shadow of his hand
Falls from his desk onto the wall
And is the only thing that moves
Anywhere at all.

Or else he will drive back at night
To walk along the corridor
And, thinking of the day's success,
Trace his steps once more.

Then pause in a darkened stairway
Until the sounds of his steps have ceased
And stroke the wall as if it were
Some attendant beast.

Racing with the Wolves

KATE BERTRAND

She never thought of power as her sport
until one night, over a business drink,
the sporting urge emerged. She played the flirt
to lure her lean, grey boss. And in a wink
the race was on. She hurdled past his wiles—
created charming lies, gazed in his eyes.
Of course he wrote no memo for the files,
describing nylon foot on flannel thigh
or trysts at noon. But someone did, and though
the wolf was quick, he fell behind. The race
was hers, the corner office, teak desk. No
more rendezvous—with him. The faster pace
agreed with her. The hungry young run fast,
until their youth and hunger fade, at last.

I'm Late Again

TONY RIZZO

The train limped into Mamaroneck
thirty minutes late
and crawled to Grand Central.
Now the bus is tripping
at every traffic light on 2nd Avenue.

If I had taken the subway,
it would have stumbled
into the wrong tunnel.

Jam

TONY RIZZO

I'm caught in a quandary these days.
I work more at home than I do at work.
And the only repose in my miserable life
is this Gordian jam.
Could it be?
All these people, like me,
looking forward each way
to the jam of the day?

The Betrayal

TONY RIZZO

Swim now or swim later, these are my choices.
I can jump and head for land,
Or I can wait until I'm pushed,
Try to make it with the crowd.

Damn the helmsman!
We all could see the storm,

He knew this boat was overloaded,
And he didn't head for land.

There he sits, his life-vest on.
Does he not feel the wind?
Why does he polish his damned bucket,
His brass bucket?

Outplacement Blues

CONSTANCE ALEXANDER

1.
Welcome to world
headquarters, the command
and control center
of the corporation.
My name is Hal Fulmer
and you'll have to
pardon my appearance.
I think I'm having
a nervous breakdown,
even though they don't
call it that any more.
It's stress.
Workplace-induced anxiety.
Job misery.
Employment uncertainty.
Career panic.
Vocational anomie.
The corporation,
you see,
is in the midst of
downsizing
resizing
right-sizing
redesigning
restructuring

reshaping
reapproximating
reorganizing
retrofitting
reshuffling the boxes
playing the blue chip version
of three card monte
sketching the new
infrastructure
on the back of a
cocktail napkin
so we can be
lean and mean.
Like assassins.
Wild dogs.
A marathon runner
with PMS.

2.
As we get ready
to meet the challenges
of the future
we are determined
to hit the ground running.
Sharpen the edge
of our competitive advantage.
Strive for excellence.
Thrive on chaos.
Swim with the sharks.
Play games our mothers
never taught us.
Learn what they don't teach
at the Harvard Business School.
Pull our own strings.
Be our own best friends.
Get to yes.
Take the less traveled road.

Mistake our wives for our hats.
This is what happens
when you hit the ground running.
Sorry.
It's just too much for me.

3.
My name is Hal Fulmer
and I'm going to kill myself
with this gun I bought so my wife,
ex-wife, excuse me,
could protect herself
while I was away on
business trips, working
on corporate strategy
so the company could take
an aggressive stance
in an increasingly competitive
worldwide marketplace.
My name is Hal
and I've been designated
for outplacement.
Early retirement.
VIPP—the voluntary incentive
placement program—
sounds like a laxative.
Or is it MOPP—
management outsizing protection plan?

No matter.
Officially, I'm dead meat.
Day old bread.
Surplus.
Like the cheese they give
welfare mothers.
An unmarked box of greasy Velveeta
you're supposed to be grateful for.

Think of me as excess protein,
a little fat to be trimmed
from the corporate gut.

I'm taking it well,
don't you think?
Had the gun all day
and didn't kill anyone.
Aimed at a few
when no one was looking
but managed to restrain myself.

Could've had a VP of marketing
on the jogging path,
a division manager of
transmission systems
at the urinal.
But I decided to
hold off. Or hold on.
Until I thought it through.
If I play my cards right,
my story'll get on Oprah
or Donahue. God! I'd
love to see Phil leaping through
the audience, railing against
the cold corporate heart.
Can't you hear him?

"Do you mean to tell me,
Mr. High-and-Mighty Executive,
that you can actually sleep at night
when you're laying off thousands
of loyal employees with a limp handshake
and a couple of months' pay?"
God! I love that silver hair, the self-righteousness,
the rage of a fallen Catholic who still believes
in purgatory. Phil could do a nice job
with my case.

He'll interview some personnel types,
who will swear that the company's
E.A.P.—excuse me, Employee Assistance Program—
was fully equipped to deal with depression
and the other aftermath of—ahem—restructuring.
Phil'll shove that microphone right into their faces
and give that cross-eyed stare that says, "You've got to
be outta your mind."

But instead he'll whisper to the guy,
probably spitting a little,
still smelling of last night's Scotch and Marlo:
"You mean to say that no one, not one single person
in that well educated group of—
of masters of the universe—
anticipated that Hal Fulmer
might blow out his brains at sunrise on the morning
his so-called outplacement took effect?"
By now, Phil's quivering.
His upper lip glistens with sweat.
He's on a roll.
"Not one of your hot-shot MBA types,
excuse me, masters of business administration geniuses,
predicted that this sensitive, lonely man would—
in a desperate bid to get the attention
of your top level executives—
commit suicide in the very headquarters building
that was really his home for seventeen years?
Why, in the note he said he spent more time in the office
than he ever spent in the house he bought for himself
and his lovely wife, excuse me, ex-wife, Brenda."

Yeah. That's how it'd go.
I wonder if—no, Brenda wouldn't consent
to an interview.
She hates Donahue.
Oprah, maybe.

No matter what,
my secretary'll
defend me.
And maybe the janitorial staff.
"Nice guy," they'll say.
"Always wrote 'Don't erase'
in big purple letters
on his whiteboard."
And maybe my cousin Harry'll
say what a regular guy I was.
"Loved the Dodgers. Hated
that they moved outta Brooklyn.
Never got over it."
That's what
he'll say.
That stuff.

Jenkins Is A-Weeping

MICHAEL IVENS

Unaccustomed as he was
To public speaking, laughing, crying, dancing,
Singing, or other extravagances
Better left undone, or second best,
Released in the private bar or in the home,
He found that,
          "Retirement is a bit of a shock,
I'm going to miss all my colleagues and friends,
And thank you so much for this wonderful clock
And ..."
                    Heard a curious song
                         And stopped.

"Tick, tock, tick, tock.
Time has gone to where and what?
Time has gone and Time has come
And what do we do to fill in Time?"

Poor Jenkins has stopped speaking,
Has stopped speaking,
Has stopped speaking,
Poor Jenkins has stopped speaking
On his bright leaving day.

Ignoring the song and ignoring the pain
He started to make his speech again.
"I remember the day I joined the firm,
The air was bright,
The grass was firm,
I felt like a gay and turning worm
And never regretted joining the firm
For a single day,
Not, of course, that it was just the pay,
It was my friends who gave me this wonderful clock,
Tick, tock, tick, tock . . ."
                              And stopped.

Poor Jenkins is a weeping,
Is a weeping,
Is a weeping,
Poor Jenkins is a weeping
On his bright leaving day.

Don Juan in a Dark Suit

MICHAEL IVENS

Don Juan in a dark suit;
Miss Leporello guarding his phones.
Typing his notes, announcing him "tied up
At a conference." Too self conscious to recite

His list of victims, he fears no Commander
But a divorce court judge and a careless abortionist.

The technique? Simple. A curious picture.
Absolutely blank, hung on the wall of his interesting bedroom.
"Sit just there please while I get it down." He removes
The picture which is unusually heavy
And holds it up, his heart and muscles bursting with the strain.

"Now look closer." She peers and straight away is lost.
What does she see? Something she can never quite explain.
Unique, vague, shifting, tender and beautiful.
Perhaps tragic. And he sees nothing,
Only the beauty and committal in her face.

Pending

MICHAEL IVENS

A filing cabinet
higher than Everest
labelled
"lives pending"

An in-tray
deeper than doubt;
"Hopes
    forgotten"

The basket
littered with regrets:
love's
    flawed carbon copies

Waiting

JONATHAN PRICE

I am here with the ferns, fast gusts
Blowing frond and stern bang into the plate glass. Click
Go the beams as weight shifts, the corporation walks
Above me, and outside, backhoes beep backing up,
Tearing San Jose farm land into condo lots, acres
Of fake villas suddenly replacing corn. This wind
Scratches and rubs the Japanese maple against the window,
Restless, passionate in a small space, invisible
As emotion, fluidly starting to destroy
This block of integrated circuits, this sea of gates,
This array of pins, wires, nets, and property lists.
The company name is Cadence; its beat of logic
Gouges a path for electrons, turns symbol
Into schematic, compressing years of code in one
Thin wafer, with gold prongs. Mozart's a product,
Striking arpeggios out of silicon. I pull the blinds
To block out the view of people entering, and float,
Within my conference room, clean and cold.

I'll Be Home at Six (a promise I will keep)

PATRICIA BROWN

Today I made a promise
   the kind one keeps if sincere,
   broken when priorities lie elsewhere.

Some live by promises;
   others never enter into them.
I am the latter changing to the former.
   A most radical move; a forfeited risk.

My spouse utters ultimatums
  "On time, any time, you chose the
  time,
  but you're held to that time!" (or
  else?)
Most demanding, threatening, yet
  reasonable.

But the work deadlines disagree.
  They also utter ultimatums
"It must be done, time is of the essence,
  lost if late." (or else?)
Most demanding, threatening, yet
  unreasonable.

Timetables, some reachable, others out of
  grasp.
So unachievable, the homefront ones.
Reasoning holds that
  it shall be damned at six,
  returning home as vowed,
  a self-imposed schedule,
  my own chosen time.

And, I will hold to his pledge.
  I'll be home at six, dear,
  I'll be home at six, somehow,
  I'll be home at six (California time).

Maid Service

PATRICIA BROWN

I was contemplating
the recommendation of air freshners
or perhaps
smokeless ash trays

to the annual budget proposal
when at half past eight
Willie Mae cornered the door

Her meticulous meandering
from office to office
a bit of dusting here
some vacuuming
had deposited her right at my sanctum

As I continued my task
uninterrupted
she proceeded to tidy about
humming
organizing around me
rubbing the tables raw with her sweat

A wastebasket emptied
a bookend straightened
all without saying a word
while I attempted to ignore
this methodical maid
questioning her life as it stood

Was she happy cleaning the tables
dusting clocks
pushing a broom?
Was there purpose in her motions?
accomplishment?
a sense of respect?
Or does she dream of a life
that I'm leading
a fine office
a rug and a chair
an executive with countless privileges
who works on projects

requiring responsibility
with far reaching consequences
such as proposing air freshners
for employees who complain about
environmental work conditions

I was about to rid the silence
and offer conversation insuring
it was understood
whose office she was cleaning
but at that moment she plugged in the vacuum

I heard someone shout down the hall
                    Willie Mae, do a thorough job
                    on that one—clean it up!
                    Make sure ALL the dirt's out

As she rose from the plug
turned on the machine
and proceeded to vacuum the room
I returned to my task
attempting to ignore
the roar
the whir of it all

Then
just when I placed
the finishing touches on my craft
she started to clean at my feet

But before I could explain
I was planning to leave . . .
                    (Willie Mae
                    swept me away)

Recessions

JAMES A. AUTRY

Why do we keep on keeping on,
in the midst of such pressure,
when business is no good for no reason,
when everything done right turns out wrong,
when the Fed does something
and interest rates do something
and somebody's notion of consumer confidence does
    something
and the dogs won't eat the dog food?

What keeps us working late at night
and going back every morning,
living on coffee and waiting for things to bottom out,
crunching numbers as if some answer
lay buried in a computer
and not out among the people who
suddenly and for no reason
are leaving their money in their pockets
and the products on the shelves?

Why don't we just say screw it
instead of trying again,
instead of meandering into somebody's office
with half an idea,
hoping he'll have the other half,
hoping what sometimes happens will happen,
that thing, that click, that moment
when two or three of us
gathered together or hanging out
get hit by something we've never tried
but know we can make work the first time?

Could that be it,
that we do all the dull stuff

just for those times
when a revelation rises among us
like something borning,
a new life, another hope,
like something not visible catching the sun,
like a prayer answered?

Dialogue with the Past

JAMES A. AUTRY

What are you doing here
in this conference room
out of the cotton fields and red dust
looking over the coffee and pads
lined yellow and legal size
pretending to be a company man?
What do you expect me to think
with your country church and preacher man rightness
nodding at the plan
smiling at the chart
acting like the profit margins make a damn
when I know where you come from?
Who do you think you're kidding
the cowshit just off your shoes
not far enough from overalls
to be happy in a collar
with GQ in the briefcase
a charge at Saks
and your grandfather restless in the cemetery
every time the closet opens?

Wait wait
I'm the same and it is too
and nothing changes but the words

When the CEO shuffles his feet
in their Italian leather loafers
and calls for further study
and appoints a task force
it's one of the county supervisors
in overalls and brogans
kicking the dust and saying
well fellers sometimes I think, well
then again I just don't know
And everybody goes off and thinks about it some more

But what are you trying to prove
when you didn't have a pot to pee in
or a window to throw it out of
when the roof leaked and the rats came in
and you looking now to shelter
your money as well as yourself?

Only that I still want what I wanted
when you cut through the shit
to do to get to hang on to something
and I only made the trade
country church for conference room
deacons for directors
and chicken in the pot for a few shares of stock

Genealogy

JAMES A. AUTRY

You are
in these hills
who you were and who you will become
and not just who you are
> *She was a McKinstry*
> *and his mother was a Smith*

And the listeners nod
at what the combination will produce
those generations to come
of thievery or honesty
of heathens or Christians
of slovenly men or working
      'Course her mother was a Sprayberry
And the new name rises
to the shaking of heads
the tightening of lips
the widening of eyes
      And his daddy's mother was a McIlhenney
Oh god a McIlhenney
and silence prays for the unborn children
those little McKinstry Smith Sprayberry McIlhenneys
      Her daddy was no count and her daddy's daddy was no count
Old Brother Jim Goff said it
when Mary Allen was pregnant
      Might's well send that chile
      to the penitentiary soon he's born
      gonna end up there anyway
But that lineage could also forgive
with benign expectation
of transgressions to come
      'Course, what do you expect
      his granddaddy was a Wilkins
      The Whitsells are a little crazy
      but they generally don't beat up nobody outside the family
      You can't expect much work out of a Latham
      but they won't steal from you
In other times and other places
there are new families and new names
      He's ex P & G
      out of Benton and Bowles
      and was brand management with Colgate
And listeners sip Dewar's and soda or puff New True Lights
and know how people will do things

they are expected to do
New fathers spring up and new sons and grandsons
always in jeopardy of leaving the family
    Watch young Dillard
    if he can work for Burton he's golden
    but he could be out tomorrow
And new marriages are bartered for old-fashioned reasons
    If you want a direct marketing guy
    get a headhunter after someone at Time Inc.
Through it all
communities new and old watch and judge and make sure
the names are in order
and everyone understands

On Firing a Salesman

JAMES A. AUTRY

It's like a little murder,
taking his life,
his reason for getting on the train,
his lunches at Christ Cella,
and his meetings in warm and sunny places
where they all gather,
these smiling men,
in sherbet slacks and blue blazers,
and talk about business
but never about prices,
never breaking that law
about the prices they charge.

But what about the prices they pay?
What about gray evenings in the bar car
and smoke-filled clothes and hair
and children already asleep
and wives who say

"You stink"
when they come to bed?
What about the promotions they don't get,
the good accounts they lose
to some kid MBA
because somebody thinks their energy is gone?

What about those times they see in a mirror
or the corner of their eye
some guy at the club shake his head
when they walk through the locker room
the way they shook their heads years ago
at an old duffer
whose handicap had grown along with his age?

And what about this morning,
the summons,
the closed door,
and somebody shaved and barbered and shined
fifteen years their junior
trying to put on a sad face
and saying he understands?

A murder with no funeral,
nothing but those quick steps outside the door,
those set jaws,
those confident smiles,
that young disregard for even the thought
of a salesman's mortality.

The Jubilar*

FRITZ KORNFELD

He who serves and perseveres
Inevitably, come what may,

*Jubilar: In Germany, a person celebrating a special 25th/40th anniversary at work or the office.

Will wake to laurels round his ears
And be our "Jubilar" one day.
Yet what he may have done to earn it
May not spring at once to mind;
The more we struggle to discern it,
The more suspicions we may find.

Did he not, with others sweating,
Weary, sore hands, strength all gone,
Sit idly by, alone regretting
Such pressures on his sit-upon?
Did he not, with poker cunning,
Play his cards behind the scenes,
Pusillanimously shunning
Other jobs by any means?

Easy now, you friendly sceptics.
Show some justice to the man.
Though work exchange sent him dyspeptic,
Do make the best case that you can.

Surely he did more than shirking,
Wearing thin his seat-of-pants?
Tyrannising others working,
Crawling with the sycophants?

Surely more than mere kow-towing
Shoved him forward, inch by inch,
And through his office slumbers knowing
Other hands were at the winch?

Was it for his presence merely
That his cheques came? Think again.
Surely there was something really
Bright he did, just now and then.

Translated from the German
by Inge Adams and Ralph Windle

The City

JOHN BETJEMAN

Business men with awkward hips
And dirty jokes upon their lips,
And large behinds and jingling chains,
And riddled teeth and riddling brains,
And plump white fingers made to curl
Round some anaemic city girl,
And so lend colour to the lives
And old suspicions of their wives.

Young men who wear on office stools
The ties of minor public schools,
Each learning how to be a sinner
And tell "a good one" after dinner,
And so discover it is rather
Fun to go one more than father.
But father, son and clerk join up
To talk about the Football Cup.

Business Girls

JOHN BETJEMAN

From the geyser ventilators
    Autumn winds are blowing down
On a thousand business women
    Having baths in Camden Town.

Waste pipes chuckle into runnels,
    Steam's escaping here and there,
Morning trains through Camden cutting
    Shake the Crescent and the Square.

Early nip of changeful autumn,
   Dahlias glimpsed through garden doors,
At the back precarious bathrooms
   Jutting out from upper floors;

And behind their frail partitions
   Business women lie and soak,
Seeing through the draughty skylight
   Flying clouds and railway smoke.

Rest you there, poor unbelov'd ones,
   Lap your loneliness in heat.
All too soon the tiny breakfast,
   Trolley-bus and windy street!

Bizness Song

ANONYMOUS

My typist has Gone on hir holliday
My tipyst has gohn on a spree
Mx typish hap gone on hyr haliduy
   o grinbacq m! hypysh tu me*

   Bling bac? OK£ring back
   oh bynk b4ck my tipisth tomi tu mee
   Brung bicq, oc sling 8@ck
   oe blynk ba"=k my T#py%? tp m6-

The Business Consultant

BERTIE RAMSBOTTOM

Of all the businesses, by far,
Consultancy's the most bizarre!
For, to the penetrating eye,
There's no apparent reason why
This group of personable men—
With no more assets than a pen—
Can sell to clients more than twice
The same ridiculous advice;
Or find, in such a rich profusion,
Problems to fit their own solution!

The strategy that they pursue—
To give advice instead of do—
Keeps their fingers on the pulses
Without recourse to stomach ulcers;
And brings them monetary gain,
Without a modicum of pain.

The wretched object of their quest,
Reduced to cardiac arrest,
Is left alone to implement
The asinine report they've sent.
Meanwhile the analysts have gone
Back to client number one,
Who desperately needs more aid
To tidy up the mess they made.
And on and on—ad infinitum—
The masochistic clients invite 'em,
Until the Merciful Reliever
Invokes the Corporate Receiver.

No one really seems to know
The rate at which consultants grow;
By some amoeba-like division?
Or chemo-biologic fission?
They clone themselves without an end
Along their exponential trend.

The paradox is each adviser,
Should he make some client wiser,
Might inadvertently destroy
The basis of his future joy;
So, does anybody know
Where latter day consultants go?

Lady on the Board

BERTIE RAMSBOTTOM

A boardroom is a kind of den
Wholly redolent of men,
Which women mainly get to see
When bringing in the lunch or tea;
But one or two, I would applaud,
Have brought a Lady on the Board,
Either out of great acumen
Or as their "statutory woman."

Either way, the eye detects
Unexpected side effects,
That tend to make the boardroom rock
To massive metabolic shock,
And leave the gentlemen regretting
A problem of their own begetting.

For here the chauvinistic mind
Seems inescapably inclined

To place, in two main categories,
The ladies central to their worries;
Disparaging, behind their backs,
Their "bomb-shell" or their "battle-ax."

The "bomb-shell" image is a figure
Like Marilyn Monroe's, but bigger—
Elegant, but only just,
Clothed about the thighs and bust;
Offering like Eliot's miss
Some promise of pneumatic bliss.

But contrary to male assumption
That pretty blondes have little gumption,
The modern version boasts degrees
Like MBA, and Ph.Ds,
And an intellect as real
As her physical appeal;

A combination which the men
Never hope to see again!
And, envy coupled with desire,
They watch the goddess rising higher
Until, with sunlight in her hair,
She occupies the Chairman's chair.

The "battle-ax" implies a style
More dependent on her guile,
Since her feministic facets
Are seen as insubstantial assets.
Eschewing every pleasure known,
To which the weaker men are prone,
She maddeningly seems to know
Everyone's portfolio;
And, where information's power,
Accumulates it hour by hour,
Until, by process of attrition,
She decimates the opposition.

These ancient overtones of sex
Cannot prevent what happens next,
When every boardroom stands ajar
To women as they really are—
Good and bad, like all the others
Of their gentlemanly brothers;
Revealing—and it really hurts—
The irrelevancy of their skirts!

Dolor

THEODORE ROETHKE

I have known the inexorable sadness of pencils,
Neat in their boxes, dolor of pad and paper-weight,
All the misery of manilla folders and mucilage,
Desolation in immaculate public places,
Lonely reception room, lavatory, switchboard,
The unalterable pathos of basin and pitcher,
Ritual of multigraph, paper-clip, comma,
Endless duplication of lives and objects.
And I have seen dust from the walls of institutions,
Finer than flour, alive, more dangerous than silica,
Sift, almost invisible, through long afternoons of tedium,
Dropping a fine film on nails and delicate eyebrows,
Glazing the pale hair, the duplicate grey standard faces.

Out of Place

WILLIAM OXLEY

The air-conditioned typists
and appalling clerks
with mongrel twangs
like wind catching
in taut telephone wires.

I watch dirigible clouds
creep round sugar-cube-
and-glass buildings
thinking: Where's
the bloody sun?

The dance of high
finance, bad colds,
O City bitter as coffee
where does one
interface with reality?

Nothing so comfortable
as nothing here
save, let's face it
man, in an office
you're out of place.

I Am Getting a Mountain View

FLOYD SKLOOT

The men have come again to move partitions.
They are working their way back and toward
my present work station and should be ready for me
by Thursday. I am getting a mountain view,
a station by the eastern windows and far enough
north to see around the stair tube and smoke tower balcony.

My phone already rings over there. When people call me,
I get While You Were Out messages within the hour
and can return their calls from the phone that used to be mine,
still on the credenza I have labeled with my name.
Everything goes and is labeled. You can never tell.
They moved Wayne when he was on break
and he still can't find his map of the state.

The old way to the copy room and the coffee pot
has been blocked by file cabinets but there are worse hazards,
like raised outlets exposed, holes where phone cables were,
chairs in aisles, desks on dollies and movers lunging
blindly behind a load of shelves. I can hardly work
with all the hammering and chatting.

People have been leaving for lunch early
and going home at four. But not me.
I think that's why I am getting a mountain view,
because I have always worked with such concentration.
In fact, I want to be sure to hang my poster of *Le Thermogène*
first thing on the wall behind me because
it depicts so accurately my way of doing business.

A Working Marriage

FLOYD SKLOOT

No hardy phlox or spice pinks in neat rows.
Ragged lawn with untrimmed hedge, wasted space,
no garden. One more sultry spring. No time
for rest, day and night thick with choice. Nothing
on the wind but must, nothing in the way
of movement. The one truth is urgency.

Up at five, worksheets still spread. Urgency
wafting like smoke wakes the spouse. Two rows
of claret stains trickling down the stairway
mark their path to bed. Coffee brews. No space
for cups, no hunger or chitchat. Nothing
to be gained by touching; there may be time

later. They work in separate rooms, time
showers around toast and the urgency
of soft-boiled eggs. Outside, jays with nothing
to stop them seize the backyard, their harsh row

almost distracting. Squirrels spring through space
a phone cable makes in elm leaves. The way

one's tail twitches before she runs away
makes her mate move through leaves like wind. No time
to lose, nothing on paper yet but space,
nothing quite as clear as the urgency
to look back from the window, start a row
of words down another sheet with nothing

on it. There are needs to project. Nothing
adds up. Footsteps of their child are the way
they know morning is relative. His row
of days leads mark by mark toward summertime,
weeks squandered, play the only urgency.
He eats toast and cheese in a cleared space

among flowcharts, ignoring the tense space
before the rush to scatter. Now nothing
can wait. Lights and locks. All is urgency.
Briefcase and thermos, hugs on the driveway,
all words becoming a matter of time.

They use sidestreets to bypass docile rows
of cars in their way, quick turns to make time.
Nothing can compete with the urgency
of desks without free space, stacks in long rows.

The Office Christmas Party

ANNE LONG

The party started happily
With a festive word or two
From the Chairman of the company
To his very merry crew
There's wine and beer and special punch

Concocted by "Design"
That's guaranteed to make things swing
In the minimum of time
With crackers pulled and paper hats
And streamers everywhere
There's even yards of silly string
In Arthur Pringle's hair
George has got his arm around
Miss Whittaker, no less
And someones being naughty
In a strapless, backless dress
Jim and Doris from Accounts
Have slipped away unseen
And there's noises in the typing pool
Behind the soundproof screen
The punch has proved a touch too strong
For many of sales aces
And its stripey tigers in the loos
And quite a few green faces
Next week when all come back to work
Some won't want to remember
What they did at party time
On the 19th of December.

Merrill Lynch

EMILY HAWTHORNE

Young scion
of a food chain family
collar and feet too large
sits in a meeting about a new stock offering
Mauna Loa Macadamia Nuts
He raises his hand:

"Shouldn't we be concerned about the amount of cholesterol
        in each nut?"
Everyone laughs.

I am in a meeting
more sales training for young brokers.
A manager without an office
is visiting ours.
He is speaking about motivation:
"Unless you know what you want and go for it,
        you might as well blow your brains out."
He has no office to manage
and his wife has left him.

I am walking down the hall
thinking about lunch and how much I hate nylons.
My big ticket has been noticed
My manager's been friendly toward me all morning
He's visiting the two big hitters in a corner office
Some male bonding, I think.

He motions for me to drop by
this is quite an honor.
I walk in and say hello.
(The usual greeting is more casual)
Four smiling white men turn to me
nails polished, hair trim

The manager without an office
bares his teeth
"Hey Emily, nice ticket. Where are your knee pads?"
Judging from the laughter
this is quite funny.

I am on hold
watching the quotron blink, office babel buffeting me.
A lull, then cries of disbelief
Someone runs heavily past my cubicle

The quotron news service explains in one line
"The space shuttle Challenger exploded 71 seconds after takeoff."
Then some news about coffee prices.

I hang up. Find an office with a television
Usually it scrolls numbers in black and white
now showing, over and over
an arcing smoke trail
then a lopsided chrysanthemum.
The sound is an announcer's grim voice I can't understand
Above the drone, in the tiny dark room, several brokers
        are already trying to outdo each other.
"I'll bet it was the teacher! Pushed the wrong button!"
I can't hear the announcer so I tell them to shut up.

One turns to me:
"Lighten up, Emily."

Testimonial

HARRY NEWMAN, JR.

You are cordially invited
To attend, at $100 a plate
A testimonial to those
Who have devoted their lives
Unstintingly
Unselfishly
To the humanitarian purpose
Of making money.

No sacrifice too great
No relationship too dear
To accumulate enough
To afford the luxury

Of giving it away
In some worthy cause
Or other.

Just listen to that applause
From the thousand or more
Gathered here in tribute,
Black tied, bejeweled,
Pledging their allegiance
To the honorees and
To the secret hope
That one such memorable night
They too might step
Into the blue-white shaft
And receive their plaque.

Survival Kit

HARRY NEWMAN, JR.

Eat your vitamins
Jog three times a week
Work out at the gym
Follow that salt-free
Low-cholesterol diet
Religiously

Bend all your efforts
To survive
And in the process
You will forget about
Living

Business Friends

HARRY NEWMAN, JR.

Cultivating a friend in business
Is tightrope walking in a gale

If you have something to gain
And use your friendship
As a moral lever
For achieving it,
You have placed a price tag
Of no value
On your relationship,
And in the process
Made you and it, not him,
A whore

If you have the strength
To elevate your friendship
Above the marketplace
And invest it with yourself,
No matter what the outcome
At the bargaining table,
Then you have created
Something lasting, life-enhancing
And rare

What Do You Want to Hear?
or
The Ideal Salesman

HARRY NEWMAN, JR.

If I can banish my identity
And substitute his for mine,
If I can play Boswell to his Johnson
And have him take my ingenuity as his,

If I can be a gilt-tongued chameleon
Attuned, litmus-like, to his every mood,
If I can manipulate him, unaware,
To my predetermined ends,

Steely-eyed above a smiling mouth
Uttering hypnotic, well-modulated sounds
Simulating warmth and understanding

Then I will achieve
The ultimate perfection—
Control

And all I sacrifice
In the process
Is myself

Kindly Unhitch That Star, Buddy

OGDEN NASH

One beacon doth their paths illumine.
To wit: To err is always humine.

I hardly suppose I know anybody who wouldn't rather be a
success than a failure,

Just as I suppose every piece of crabgrass in the garden would
much rather be an azalea,

And in celestial circles all the run-of-the-mill angels would rather
be archangels or at least cherubim and seraphim,

And in the legal world all the little process-servers hope to grow
up into great big bailiffim and sheriffim.

Indeed, everybody wants to be a wow,

But not everybody knows exactly how.

Some people think they will eventually wear diamonds instead of
rhinestones

Only by everlastingly keeping their noses to their ghrinestones,

And other people think they will be able to put in more time at
Palm Beach and the Ritz

By not paying too much attention to attendance at the office but
rather in being brilliant by starts and fits.

Some people after a full day's work sit up all night getting a
college education by correspondence,

While others seem to think they'll get just as far by devoting their
evenings to the study of the difference in temperament between
brunettance and blondance.

In short, the world is filled with people trying to achieve success,

And half of them think they'll get it by saying No and half of
them by saying Yes,

And if all the ones who say No said Yes, and vice versa, such is the
fate of humanity that ninety-nine percent of them still wouldn't
be any better off than they were before,

Which perhaps is just as well because if everybody was a success
    nobody could be contemptuous of anybody else and everybody
    would start in all over again trying to be a bigger success than
    everybody else so they would have somebody to be
    contemptuous of and so on forevermore,
Because when people start hitching their wagons to a star,
That's the way they are.

Canto VI

Comings
and Goings

Kindly allow me to be your tutor.
I wish to explain about the commuter.
 —Ogden Nash, *The Banker's Special*

Getting off to travel far he leaves her;
She remains withdrawn,
Watching him away to touch a
   thousand hands.
 —Brian Smith, *Travelling Man*

Off again
in all directions
like a chicken with his head cut off...
 —James A. Autry, *Off Again*

The Complete De-Anxietised Man

BRIAN SMITH

Seven four seven
And seven miles high in polar blue.
Extravaganza USA.
A score of ice-cold hostesses.
A captain "overheading Glass-gow"
On the short route to Los Angeles.

The menu. French.
Is genuine American:
The films are British
And just as insincere.

But channel nine
On stereo gives something real:
Pink Floyd. The Who and Love.
The Jimi Hendrix Collage,
Charlie Haden's Liberation—
Saying with a common depth
Of understanding what I feel
Is truly here at seven up.

What Do I Want with Paris?

BRIAN SMITH

Stalking the world with a
    business proboscis.
Hazarding guilt if your motives
    should wander;

Keeping your senses awake and akimbo,
Hoping to find them uniquely responsive;

Fearing conventional travellers' jargon,
Leary of everything others have done:

Late here in Paris, your nerve-endings
   thriving,
Fate sits in waiting to grab you
   —but where?

Travelling Man

BRIAN SMITH

Getting off to travel far he leaves her;
She remains withdrawn,
Watching him away to touch a
   thousand hands.

But now he binds himself within his
   own cocoon.
Indulging introvertedly.
She, unchained within her local
   cage, takes flight.

707 to Nassau

BRIAN SMITH

This is the good life—
Here the clouds of insubstantial snow,
Here the engines stark defined against
   a new-found space.
This is the time.
Here the wine, the oh so super over-spent promotion,
Chickens' livers, caviar and champagne;

Hours to spare,
This is the present I wanted,
This is the time, the instant
Built from months of preview,
Months of recollection—
This is the time,
Months of preview do I say?
A minute means the same,
How to keep the moment—
Write and draw and photograph;
Sit intense and concentrate;
But it will go.

Aging Jet Setter

HARRY NEWMAN, JR.

I search the mirror's silvered eye
Strange faces stare, mere passersby.
But where am I?
Where am I?

They touch my life with ready hand
Well-mannered, gilt-edged, night-bulb tanned.
But what of me?
What of me?

I give myself with caviar and wines
Revere the aged, but reject the aging lines.
But what have I?
What have I?

Wealth and envy and well-cut suits
A mocking love from glossy brutes.
But who am I?
Who am I?

Again I search the mirror's darkening eye.
I see an image passing by
Of a kindly and a gentle mien
Seeking courage to be seen.
Love yourself, it says, for what you are,
Ere time snuffs out your life's own star.

Out of Synch

HARRY NEWMAN, JR.

I mark the passing of time
Not by night and day
The pulsing of the tides
The masking of the moon
The rusting of the maple leaf
The rebirth of the rose

But by apppointments
Plane schedules
And deadlines
Superimposing their own
Artificial chronology
On time
And my ever-changing moods

Awake

HARRY NEWMAN, JR.

Damn!
It's four thirty
And I'm awake.
The internal clockwork
Has sounded its false alarm.

It's always the same
In Seattle, Chicago
Or New York.

Like an accusing finger
The endless list unfolds
Of too much to do
And too much undone.

The adrenalin of
Recrimination
Speeds the brain.
The acid taste of
Anxiety
Knots my gut.

The Kafka trial begins
My only plea is guilt
My defense self-doubt
My best hope, acquittal
By the hung jury of sleep.

But if the past is any guide
The sentence will be suspended
Until the next indictment is returned
Tomorrow night.

Notes Taken on a Business Trip

JIM LINDOP

ATLANTA—GEORGIA
Fretful
assymetry of
men and masonry:
a manic Legoland

that sulks,
brooded by
a minatory rain.
This carious city
bleeds
its high-class past
across
its moping
now.

LOS ANGELES AIRPORT

Delta Tristar,
big tin manta,
flopped down through the
scrim of smog that
shawled the sprawling
lax, lax city;
then on tip-toe
extruded out
its human kelp
into this gimcrack
scullery.
Here tawdry
is finesse—
and happiness
is a suntan
and a Sony Walkman.

HONG KONG

Hustler city,
sea-salved,
and at its back
a bridled dragon
seething.

Business Connection

CHARLES BLACKBURN OWEN

Slipping down the Vale from Hampstead,
  Camel coat and fat cigar,
Hub-caps sparking winter sunshine,
  Sunshine on your Jaguar,

Eyes still hold the old suspicion,
  Rosy corpulence conceals
Years of roller-coaster fortunes,
  Bitten nails and knife-edge deals,

Not for you the careful luncheons,
  Dieticians tracts or pills,
Port and pheasant, plump and pleasant,
  Wait for you in West End grills,

Snug behind electric windows,
  Does the planet's muted cry
Penetrate the rich Havana,
  What to sell or hold or buy?

Four o'clock will find your chauffeur
  Dozing, parked in Chelsea Green,
Polly patting back her make-up,
  Next appointment five fifteen.

Commuter Platform

CHARLES BLACKBURN OWEN

Divided love, divided care,
Synthesized at half-past eight,
  Urgency is down the stair,
Through the door and garden gate.

Platform One, time to spare
To corner, kill the rebel thought,
   To love your neighbour, to compare
His shadow pale or long or short,
   A half-way house to nowhere new,
A precognition of decay
   Before the hearse that bears us to
Another unheroic day.

The Banker's Special

OGDEN NASH

Kindly allow me to be your tutor.
I wish to explain about the commuter.
He rises so early and abrupt
That the robins complain he wake them upped.
Commuters think nothing could be more beautiful
Than the happy hours of the life commutiful,
But as one who tried it and now repentest,
I'd rather go twice a day to the dentist.
You struggle into the city's strife
With a shopping list from your thoughtful wife.
You repeat to yourself, as the day begins:
One charlotte russe; dozen bobby pins—
And then on the homeward trip you find
That this trifling chore has slipped your mind,
And the brilliantest explanation is useless
When you're bobby-pinless and charlotte russeless.
Let me add, to conclude this pitiful ditty,
A commuter is one who never knows how a show comes
   out because he has to leave early to catch a train
   to get him back to the country in time to catch a
   train to bring him back to the city.

In Cheever Country

DANA GIOIA

Half an hour north of Grand Central
the country opens up. Through the rattling
grime-streaked windows of the coach, streams appear,
pine trees gather into woods, and the leaf-swept yards
grow large enough to seem picturesque.

Farther off smooth parkways curve along the rivers,
trimmed by well-kept trees, and the County Airport
now boasts seven lines, but to know this country
see it from a train—even this crowded local
jogging home half an hour after dark

smelling of smoke and rain-damp shoes
on an afternoon of dodging sun and showers.
One trip without a book or paper
will show enough to understand
this landscape no one takes too seriously.

The architecture of each station still preserves
its fantasy beside the sordid tracks—
defiant pergolas, a shuttered summer lodge,
a shadowy pavilion framed by high-arched windows
in this land of northern sun and lingering winter.

The town names stenciled on the platform signs—
Clear Haven, Buller Park, and Shady Hill—
show that developers at least believe in poetry
if only as a talisman against the commonplace.
There always seems so much to guard against.

The sunset broadens for a moment, and the passengers
standing on the platform turn strangely luminous
in the light streaming from the palisades across the river.
Some board the train. Others greet their arrivals
shaking hands and embracing in the dusk.

If there is an afterlife, let it be a small town
gentle as this spot at just this instant.
But the car doors close, and the bright crowd,
unaware of its election, disperses to the small
pleasures of the evening. The platform falls behind.

The train gathers speed. Stations are father apart.
Marble staircases climb the hills where derelict estates
glimmer in the river-brightened dusk.
Some are convents now, some orphanages,
these palaces the Robber Barons gave to God.

And some are merely left to rot where now
broken stone lions guard a roofless colonnade,
a half-collapsed gazebo bursts with tires,
and each detail warns it is not so difficult
to make a fortune as to pass it on.

But splendor in ruins is splendor still,
even glimpsed from a passing train,
and it is wonderful to imagine standing
in the balustraded gardens above the river
where barges still ply their distant commerce.

Somewhere upstate huge factories melt ore,
mills weave fabric on enormous looms,
and sweeping combines glean the cash-green fields.
Fortunes are made. Careers advance like armies.
But here so little happens that is obvious.

Here in the odd light of a rainy afternoon
a ledger is balanced and put away,
a houseguest knots his tie beside a bed,
and a hermit thrush sings in the unsold lot
next to the tracks the train comes hurtling down.

Finally it's dark outside. Through the freight houses
and oil tanks the train begins to slow
approaching the station where rows of travel posters

and empty benches wait along the platform.
Outside a few cars idle in the sudden shower.

And this at last is home, this ordinary town
where the lights on the hill gleaming in the rain
are the lights that children bathe by, and it is time
to go home now—to drinks, to love, to supper,
to the modest places which contain our lives.

Lights Flashing at O'Hare

JAMES A. AUTRY

Taxiing in on United at O'Hare
you see fire engines and an ambulance,
lights flashing,
and you think of snowy mornings
in a trailer somewhere in France,
near a runway of accelerating sounds,
loud but comforting in their consistency.
Then nothing,
and before you remember that silence
is not what you want to hear,
that fear born of something much older than
    airplanes
rises like a siren in your brain,
who who who who who?

In your briefcase is a calendar
filled for months to come,
time stretching like a chore
as far as you can turn the pages,
another week another year
to be played out in meetings and memos and trips.
Then, looking back toward the flashing lights,
ready by the runway,

you realize that out there somewhere
some poor son of a bitch
just wants the next five minutes
to be over.

Off Again
(Reflections of the Modern Traveler)

JAMES A. AUTRY

Off again
in all directions
like a chicken with his head cut off
like a blind dog in a meat packing house
like all those things
the old people would say
if they could see me now.

It was the same
plowing a mule geeing and hawing
in the hot wet sun
sweating a spot on the porch
at dinnertime
then off again
to the slanting red fields.

It was the same
hauling fertilizer to Memphis
stopping at the Toddle House
or the Villanova where a pork chop
cost more than a steak ought to
then off again
down the black top.

It was the same
on a Greyhound bus down '78

squeezing among the uniforms and hip flasks
walking the last ten miles
past the red schoolhouse and the soapstone gully
then off again
after the cotton was picked and to the gin.

Now it's all directions at once
with an air travel card
and a carry on bag
writing a speech working a budget
sweating a meeting chewing a tums
like a chicken with his head cut off
like a blind dog in a meat packing house.

Canto VII

Politics and Power

The meek may inherit the earth—but not its mineral rights . . .
—J. Paul Getty

The businessman is the only man who is for ever apologising
   for his occupation . . .
—H. L. Mencken

The business of America is business.
—President Calvin Coolidge

The Business true-believer's Shrine
Is something called "The Bottom Line";
All Great Religions need their Sign,
Some symbol of the Most Divine.
—Bertie Ramsbottom

VIP, A Conversation

HARRY NEWMAN, JR.

I have to be there at four thirty
For a business appointment
Before a dinner meeting;
So please step on it.

What do you do, if I may ask?
He asked.

I develop shopping centers
Small ones, big ones with malls.

Oh you must really be important.

Well, I don't know about that.
How long is your shift?

You're my last fare,
I started just before noon.

What do you do the rest of the time?

Oh, I go home; only a small place
Overlooking the river,
Work my vegetable garden,
Go fishing or sailing,
Sometimes I sit and read
Or look at the mountains.

I just make enough to get along.
That's why it's so nice
To meet a successful person
Like you.

Inspector Christopher Smart Calls

PETER PORTER

Dear Friends. I have to convince you
The world you stand on is no surer
And no safer than instant pie crust.
"Instant"—yes, when the signal comes.
(Perhaps two lemon-coloured crocuses
Will flash the word across antennae,
A striped ant ferry it to our depot
Under a saw-edged tin of condensed soup),
Then it happens. What is it? Your personal
Parousia, the Biggest Show on Earth,
Meggido or bust! But until it happens
It's the breath of life to investors. And
Haven't I invested: Mrs. Midnight,
Grub Street garnishings, a seriousness
Of creditors? I warn you, don't try to turn me
Away from the door like a Jehovah's Witness.
I can put more than coupons through the crack.
I can give you sixpence off eternal fire.
Green Stamps for the furnishings of Heaven.
I'm investigating love. Holy Thrift!
What can you show me? Did you ever
Have a plan to fit metric to the psalms?
How about counting the D's in Deuteronomy,
The whole book? Too bad. Something simpler?
Perhaps a water clock that only dripped
In Advent? An hermaphrodite Pope
From the Joke Shop with working parts
To embarrass Catholic friends? A plastic
Missal leafed with Tote tickets? Come on.
There must be something mystical about you.

Did you ever lie about Sicily to your son's Headmaster?
Use your vowels on a pink paraffin man?
No joy? I'm trying to help you. Just say that once
You felt unhappy, that's how catechism starts.

Poem, or Beauty Hurts Mr. Vinal

E. E. CUMMINGS

take it from me kiddo
believe me
my country, 'tis of

you, land of the Cluett
Shirt Boston Garter and Spearmint
Girl With The Wrigley Eyes (of you
land of the Arrow Ide
and Earl &
Wilson
Collars) of you i
sing: land of Abraham Lincoln and Lydia E. Pinkham,
land above all of Just Add Hot Water and Serve—
from every B. V. D.

let freedom ring

amen. i do however protest, anent the un
-spontaneous and otherwise scented merde which
greets one (Everywhere Why) as divine poesy per
that and this radically defunct periodical. i would

suggest that certain ideas gestures
rhymes, like Gillette Razor Blades
having been used and reused
to the mystical moment of dullness emphatically are
Not To Be Resharpened. (Case in point

if we are to believe these gently O sweetly
melancholy trillers amid the thrillers
these crepuscular violinists among my and your
skyscrapers—Helen & Cleopatra were Just Too Lovely,
The Snail's On The Thorn enter Morn and God's
In His andsoforth

do you get me?) according
to such supposedly indigenous
throstles Art is O World O Life
a formula: example, Turn Your Shirttails Into
Drawers and If It Isn't An Eastman It Isn't A
Kodak therefore my friends let
us now sing each and all fortissimo A-
mer
i

ca, I
love,
You. And there're a
hun-dred-mil-lion-oth-ers, like
all of you successfully if
delicately gelded (or spaded)
gentlemen (and ladies)—pretty

littleliverpill-
hearted-Nujolneeding-There's-A-Reason
americans (who tensetendoned and with
upward vacant eyes, painfully
perpetually crouched, quivering, upon the
sternly allotted sandpile
—how silently
emit a tiny violetflavoured nuisance: Odor?

ono,
comes out like a ribbon lies flat on the brush

The Church of Business

NICK WOODWARD

The Church of Business stands supreme,
　　her towered blocks confront the sky.
Like Dante's souls her acolytes
　　grapple upon rungs of hierarchy;
Not seeking for that paradise whose milk
　　nourishes souls of humble faith
And lightens many paths to Rome,
　　transforming insubstantial life.
Green envy spurs the frantic climb
　　and dreams of power, promotion overdue,
Goad ever up the unquiet self
　　to gulp at streams of moneydew.
Bitter the taste of paradise
　　for those at last who grasp their dream—
Shadowing the graveyard of success
　　the Church of Business stands supreme.

Taking up Serpents
(Chicago Board of Trade)

LINDSAY HILL

The frenzy has the heat of religious faith
But not in the name of Christ as the darkly blessed
Hold the mouths of snakes to their bare chests
Not as the dry hot flicking tongues are prayers
This laying on of hands pretends no healing
This speaking in tongues no dialogue with Grace
Without ritual without faith
This is the spiralling center where coils lock closed
And the numbing ethers of dailiness flow pure to the heart

Ballade to a Philanthropist

G. K. CHESTERTON

You send your ships to Sunlight Port,
　Your money to Morel and Co.,
Or the Minority Report
　Or the Maternity Bureau;
　There is in all this festive flow
A point that I should like to fix,
　Your aid is shed on all below—
But will you lend me two-and-six?

You pay reformers to fall short,
　And agitators to lie low,
You pay our papers to exhort
　Our soldiers not to conquer so,
　You toss us a Town Hall at Bow
Built out of terra-cotta bricks—
　Has a Gymnasium, has it? Oh!
But will you lend me two-and-six?

I know you vetoed at Earl's Court
　That brutalising Billiard Show.
. . . Quite so . . . yes . . . yes . . . this so-called sport.
　Yes . . . so-called Christian . . . strikes a blow . . .
　Yes . . . so-called Twentieth . . . yes, I know,
. . . Degraded postures . . . player kicks
　The billiard-marker with his toe . . .
—*But will you lend me two-and-six?*

ENVOI
　Prince, I will not be knighted! No!
Put up your sword and stow your tricks!
　Offering the Garter is no go—
BUT WILL YOU LEND ME TWO-AND-SIX?

The Multinational Corporation

BERTIE RAMSBOTTOM

When James D. Flaherty O'Rourke
Came from Dublin to New York,
And peddled round his hot potatas,
Few financial commentators
Forecast he was on the brink
Of World Wide Hot Potatas Inc.,
Founding his Global Enterprise
On Chirpy Chips and Handy Fries—
But such are the bizarre gestations
Of Multinational Corporations.

And having made the humble spud
Synonymous with motherhood,
And Chips With Everything the toast
Of every home from coast to coast,
He felt that he should not deny
The culture of the Handy Fry
To less sophisticated clients,
Untutored in potato science;
And ripe, on Wall Street's best assessment,
For World Wide's overseas investment.

So soon the Hot Potata logo
Flew from Zanzibar to Togo,
With worldwide quality control
By satellite across the Pole;
Linking Chirpy Chip plantations
And process plants in fifty nations,
Including, after tense discussions,
A licence granted to the Russians.

The Tigris, Nile and Orinoco
Were switched from cotton, rice and cocoa

To propagation of the tuber,
As were tobacco farms in Cuba,
On the guaranteed assumption
Of escalating world consumption;
Till all the leading indicators
Were based on futures in potatoes,
With James the undisputed King
Of the carbohydrate Ring;
While OPEC in distress reviewed
The synthesis of starch from crude.

Wall Street analysts foretold
A flight from copper, zinc and gold,
And White House strategists demanded
Return to the Potato Standard.
Friedman joined the advocators
Of tight control of seed potatoes;
And Downing Street was quick to see
Manipulation of P3
As the relevant equation
For final conquest of inflation.

But James was keen to leave decisions
On politics to politicians,
And moved with great reluctance to
Subvert a government or two;
Executives of Hot Potatas,
Irrespective of their status
And the color of their skins,
Daily disavow their sins,
Renewing oaths to Handy Fries,
To multinational enterprise,
And James O'Rourke's financial plan
For Global Brotherhood of Man.

Death by Merger

BERTIE RAMSBOTTOM

A corporate entity, which starts
As just an aggregate of parts,
Evolves in time, within its whole,
An idiosyncratic soul.

This personality defeats
Analysis by balance sheets,
The way your character eludes
The X-ray and the cathode tubes.

These tell us much about our health,
As balance sheets of corporate wealth;
But neither takes us very far
Towards clarifying what we *are*.

But what we *are*, on this strange earth,
Defines our value and our worth;
Not, for a man, his ears or throat,
Nor, for a company, its quote.

Yet analysts are prone to make
This odd but seminal mistake,
And think the rules of purchase hold
When companies are bought or sold.

But what the buying company gets,
So often, to its great regrets,
May be a useless bag of parts,
Like buying men without their hearts.

Financial analysts are, then,
The very worst of corporate men
To make so subtle a decision
As merger or as acquisition.

This may be why we see the trail
Of acquisitions, doomed to fail,
Abandoned to the Jack-the-Rippers
Of corporate life—the asset-strippers.

Above all, it's the people presence
That permeates this corporate essence,
And catalyses, through the whole,
Its special chemistry and soul.

So synergies from mergers fail
Because the soul is not for sale;
Just as, when plants and factories close,
More dies than most of us suppose.

The United Fruit Co.

PABLO NERUDA

When the trumpet sounded, it was
all prepared on the earth,
and Jehovah parceled out the earth
to Coca-Cola, Inc., Anaconda,
Ford Motors, and other entities:
The Fruit Company, Inc.
reserved for itself the most succulent,
the central coast of my own land,
the delicate waist of America.
It rechristened its territories
as the "Banana Republics"
and over the sleeping dead,
over the restless heroes
who brought about the greatness,

the liberty and the flags,
it established the comic opera:
abolished the independencies,
presented crowns of Caesar,
unsheathed envy, attracted
the dictatorship of the flies,
Trujillo flies, Tacho flies,
Carias flies, Martinez flies,
Ubico flies, damp flies
of modest blood and marmalade,
drunken flies who zoom
over the ordinary graves,
circus flies, wise flies
well-trained in tyranny.

Among the bloodthirsty flies
the Fruit Company lands its ships,
taking off the coffee and the fruit;
the treasure of our submerged
territories flows as though
on plates into the ships.

Meanwhile Indians are falling
into the sugared chasms
of the harbors, wrapped
for burial in the mist of the dawn:
a body rolls, a thing
that has no name, a fallen cypher,
a cluster of dead fruit
thrown down on the dump.

Translated from the Spanish
by Robert Bly

Thanks to Industrial Essex

DONALD DAVIE

THANKS to industrial Essex,
I have spun on the greasy axis
Of business and sociometrics;
I have come to know the structures
Of public service
As well as I know the doves
Crop-full in mildewed haycocks.
I know that what they merit
Is not scorn, sometimes scorn
And hatred, but sadness really.

Italic on chalky tussocks,
The devious lovely weasel
Snakes through a privileged annex,
An enclave of directors.
Landscapes of supertax
Record a deathful failure
As clearly as the lack
Of a grand or expansively human
Scale to the buildings of Ilford.

The scale of that deprivation
Goes down in no statistics
536

Aphorisms

DR. LOTHAR SCHMIDT

The penny, when it drops for those in power,
Is invariably a borrowed one—and ours.
For solutions, in the politician's sense,
Are regrettably at other folk's expense.

And no matter what the economic system,
Successful politicians, when you list 'em,
Have converged like hungry sharks
On Das Kapital and Marx,
Always throwing cash at problems to resist 'em.
So beware the business economic trend
When a subsidy's a government's best friend.
Our surplus of old questions still advances,
But faster still our deficit of answers.

Translated from the German
by Inge Adams and Ralph Windle

British Conventional Guilt

BRIAN SMITH

When he thickens his skin at the Christianly meek.
When he frowns at the profit he made just this week.
When he tries to defend how his fortune was built.
—It's British conventional guilt, my friend.
    British conventional guilt.

When he builds up his ulcer with each double gin.
When he claims overweight as original sin.
When he talks of successful blood pressure prevention.
—It's British conventional guilt, my friend.
    The guilt of a British convention.

When he freezes the charm of his fair secretary,
When each lovely glimpse makes him even more wary,
When beauty itself he must write off as skittish.
—It's British conventional guilt, my friend.
    The guilt of conventional British.

Learning to Count

SIR JEREMY MORSE

Numberless son,
Let me teach you
(Or you teach me)
Your natural lore.
While we're alive
Arithmetic's
One way to heaven—
An infinite, straight
And narrow line
From God to men.

Thatcherism 1988

SIR JEREMY MORSE

The Trojan woman has out-hectored Hector
And lords it over a poor public sector
Which, grown too old to tax, holds out its hand,
Unsure whether to beg or to command.

from May, Eternal 1988

PAAVO HAAVIKKO

Life being short, poverty and wealth
   are final verdicts, in that
poverty and life are of equal duration
   and wealth and cold indifference
are perennial and hereditary, like diseases.

Translated from the Finnish by Anselm Hollo

from After the Deadline 1984

PAAVO HAAVIKKO

This is a world that will, in any case, be destroyed at some
    time.
Working for its destruction seems pointless.
It is impossible to save. Between these two facts, life has to
    be lived.
Other creatures, human and divine, differ from the mouse only by
    the frequency of their breath-rate
in and out, quickly, until you lose it.
Now, the universe is breathing out: a great breath, so that,
    from inside, it looks slow, and distant, from this edge.
When it starts breathing in, it will have breathed only once:
    out, and in.
It's time to stop recycling waste paper, it is time to stop
    producing it.
You are told that it, too, is an industry that uses up energy
    so what's it matter what you do.
And who am I if not industry and war, destruction and waste.
    I should write smaller, tell fewer lies,
get it all said, should lower my voice.

Translated from the Finnish by Anselm Hollo

Boardroom

STAFFORD BEER

I read the war poets
twice over—
that was tough. I also wrote
myself the second time round
naively.

It was a teenage party then too
but short on drugs and sex.
There was marching though,
and carrying someone's rifle
made the friend.
There was the unreal sound
half-hearted kick
of the blank cartridge
at the funerals of friends.
Looking back

we can fairly envy
the clean muck of the war,
and the bright issues
bogus but clearcut
that sorted us out
in those days.

It's different now
what with business and industry
also the academic bit.
We all storm the bridges again
London and Waterloo
doing our stuff.
But there isn't much glamour
and if you're dead by teatime
it will be
because some dolt
is driving the car, bus, taxi

or because they sacked you
and there was a mortgage.

It would be nice
shade of my best friend's ghost
to say that I went out
firing back
or crucified akimbo

in a Jap-infested sunset.
But the board now meets
and the battle I shall lose
will be over the brandy
where the teeth gnash
not rattle.

We doodle with our clickety
supersonic ball-points
while our friends
sleep and grow younger.
God, but my hair is going
and that clot
    I love him too
    and for the same reason
    that we die together
talks and talks and talks.

Canto VIII

Technolog~ and Change

Everything changes; nothing stays still.
—Heracleitus

Plus ça change, plus c'est la même chose.
The more things change, the more they stay the same.
—Jean Baptiste Alphonse Karr

Invention breeds invention...
—Ralph Waldo Emerson, *Works and Days*

Print Out: Apocalypse

PETER PORTER

When the army of ecologists
has scraped the last shellfish
from the lagoon.

When all the cars on
the urban overpasses are towed
to adventure playgrounds.

When the phrase "fossil fuel"
is considered too holy to be used
in crossword puzzles.

When 'Thirties hats and hairdos
have come back into fashion
for the tenth time.

When archivists have stored
reserve prints of every manifestation
of popular culture.

When software and hardware
have swapped places in our
advanced computers.

When these words are fed in
for me to consider. I will come again,
says the Lord . . .

Life Processors

ARIANA CLARKE

Oh give me, Lord, the WORDPERFECT life:
One I can REFORMAT at a button's touch;
Where misplaced actions are instantly JUSTIFIED;
Where the CURSOR points always to good times ahead;
Where my latest mishap's simply rectified by a touch of DELETE,
And those precious lost moments resurrected by the F1 key.

A life, above all,
whose meanings are made visible
by the simple touching of the REVEAL CODES.
The WORDPERFECT Life.

A Valentine for Christine

QUENTIN DE LA BEDOYERE

Bit by bit and byte by byte
My messages do flow;
They come by electronic flight
For Cupid's far too slow.

My quiver is a keyboard,
My disk is making tracks,
My modem's working overtime
And I send my love by fax.
XXXXX

Social Comment

WILLIAM OXLEY

More and more the right food and desperation of sex,
the healthy green with greed;
Europe heading for a one-parent-family
and then the world, U-know, the same;
intellectuals leafing *The Guardian*
their *Book of Revelation*;
hype-dependent entertainment, and taste
in poetry going the same way;
half the world playing computer games
ignoring how the other half dies,
and me—daft about syntax and daffodils—
watching the ozone holes grow
like acne on the face of tomorrow,
hearing the exhausting tune of technology
played over and over, till it's over.

New Technique

JOHN MARSH

The new technique is on its way
Thousands stop their work and pray
That it will promise nothing more
Than all the muddle seen before;
Management will beam benignly
Relying on its gifts supinely
Increasing profits while they play
At other business games—O lay!

The Medium Is the Message

BERTIE RAMSBOTTOM

The more the media expand
The less we seem to understand;
The more the information flow,
   The less we seem to think or know;
The more the messages we send,
The less we seem to comprehend;
Communication rules, OK!
   Although there's nothing much to say.

The future's Internet and cable,
Computers on the kitchen table,
With instant data through the night
   On VDU by satellite;
Let your fingers do the walking,
For who needs dialogue and talking?
Modems in the bedroom presage
   The age when media are the message.

With real-time access on the wall,
Who needs much power of speech at all?
And touch to activate retrieval
   Makes words peripherally evil.
At last our progeny are freed
From all that need to write and read,
Delivered from the old, absurd
   Tyranny of book and word.

Nor need there be much future cause
For risking it beyond the doors,
When Mum can dial beef or mutton
   By "Choose" code on the access button;
When Dad can sit at home and sell,
By hook-up on his Intertel.
And even Johnny's need to know
   Is game-boyed for his video.

The more the images we screen
The less the message comes to mean;
The more the plethora of data,
   The less the meaning seems to matter.
Maybe it's time to bequeath a
Bit less traffic on the ether,
For future ages to regain
   Some space for nourishing the brain.

We Won't Know Where We're Going Till We're There

BERTIE RAMSBOTTOM

The Times they are a-Changing,
   But not the old taboos
On asking where they're going,
   Or what it's for, and whose.

We've been M.B.O.'d and Down-Sized,
   We've been T.Q.M.'d, Divested;
Process-Cost-Re-Engineered,
   Re-Structured, Dis-Invested.
Kept up with all the "ologies,"
   Each "Go-for-Change" idea;
Read every trendy guru's book
   And business panacea;
Consorted with consultants,
   Bought their "this-should-fix-it" isms,
Gone round and round the circuits
   Of computing cataclysms.

The Times they are a-Changing,
   But not the old taboos
On asking where they're going,
   And who will get to choose.

The message is, just move it round
   Like Alice's Mad Hatter,
Back or forward, where it's bound,
   Is quite another matter.
Shake it up and slim it down
   Is mainly what enthuses;
Don't spoil the fun by asking which
   People are the losers.

So, keep the gimmicks coming, Lord,
   To save us all from needing
Such obsolescent, antique things
   As caring, thinking, leading.

Robots

KAJETAN KOVIC

The robots are on the march.

The first of them is square.
The stone it holds in its hand
Is a cube.
And a cube is forever a cube.
And all that exists is a cube.

The robots are on the march.

The second robot is round.
The stone it holds in its hand
Is a sphere.
And a sphere is forever a sphere
And all that exists is a sphere.

The robots are on the march.

The stone in the sky, the stone on the earth
Has got no choice.
Today is a stone, tomorrow a cube.
Today is a stone, tomorrow a sphere.
Today is a stone, tomorrow a robot.

The robots are on the march.

The cube smashes up the sphere.
The sphere knocks out the cube.
For a cube is forever a cube.
For a sphere is forever a sphere.

The robots are on the march.

As long as a cube is square.
As long as a sphere is round.

Engineers' Corner

WENDY COPE

Why isn't there an Engineers' Corner in Westminster
Abbey? In Britain we've always made more fuss of a
ballad than a blueprint.... How many schoolchildren
dream of becoming great engineers?
> Advertisement placed in *The Times*
> by the Engineering Council

We make more fuss of ballads than of blueprints—
That's why so many poets end up rich.
While engineers scrape by in cheerless garrets
Who needs a bridge or dam? Who needs a ditch?

Whereas the person who can write a sonnet
Has got it made. It's always been the way,
For everybody knows that we need poems
And everybody reads them every day.

Yes, life is hard if you choose engineering—
You're sure to need another job as well;
You'll have to plan your projects in the evenings
Instead of going out. It must be hell.

While well-heeled poets ride around in Daimlers.
You'll burn the midnight oil to earn a crust.
With no hope of a statue in the Abbey,
With no hope, even, of a modest bust.

No wonder small boys dream of writing couplets
And spurn the bike, the lorry and the train.
There's far too much encouragement for poets—
That's why this country's going down the drain.

Personnel in the Year 4000

ANNE LONG

One of our androids is missing
And Computer 4.9.3.0.5.
Needs a stabilised impulse intrusion
To maintain vector optimum drive

A replacement is now necessary
Approved by Alpha K. Zed
Or it will fail by implosion
When the force field goes into the red

Whole Galaxy prime requisition
Key in "Android" recruit, reconstruct
Load programmes for black holes and Saturn
Micro hours to auto-destruct

One ram megabyte from disaster
Call up programme and instigate "find"
Go to index; search Android selection
A-Alpha is almost off line

File empty, abort, press the "help" key
Go to Mars. Uranus is bare
Search Venus and Alpha Centura
The answer has got to be there

Old memory file, long forgotten
Retrieve, get it loaded, now scan
Boot up the goddam computer
The file name on this one is "MAN."

Index of Poets and Translators

Index of Titles

About the Editor

Ralph Windle is an Englishman, married to an American, and had his first insights into corporate life as an executive with two U.S. multinationals, Procter and Gamble and Nabisco.

Subsequently he became a founder fellow of Templeton College, Oxford (the Oxford Centre for Management Studies); taught and researched on several business campuses in the United States (American Graduate School of International Management, Arizona; Georgetown University and others), Switzerland and Italy; and appeared on many business conference platforms.

In more recent years he has worked as an independent strategy adviser to boards and senior managements of a number of major international businesses and institutions.

In recounting these episodes in a business life, he chooses to confess, with a wry smile, how inadequate for such a life his education might seem to some: Latin, Greek, philosophy, culminating in a "Greats" degree at Oxford. In fact, that wide and uninhibited canvass of thought, allied to a concern for words and literature, has proved central to his business life and his enjoyment and perceptions of the people in it.

His Bertie Ramsbottom verse satires—first in the *Financial Times* of London, the *Harvard Business Review*, other magazines and then books—were part of this process of reconnecting business to the mainstream of society and culture. "Only Connect" is the message he likes to send.

He is content to be known as a businessman who writes; he sees himself as a writer who is in business.

Cover Design: Casandra Chu
Illustrations: Ariana Clarke Windle
Copy Editor: Mary Lou Sumberg
Production Manager: Mary Lou Sumberg
Design and Typesetting: Harrison Typesetting, Inc.
Printer: Hamilton Printing Company
Text type: Stempel Garamond
Display type: Clairvaux
Paper: Renew Antique